HISTORIC SHIPWRECKS

Discovered, Protected & Investigated

HISTORIC SHIPWRECKS

Discovered, Protected & Investigated

Valerie Fenwick & Alison Gale

TEMPUS

First published 1998
Reprinted 1999

Published by:
Tempus Publishing Limited
The Mill, Brimscombe Port
Stroud, Gloucestershire, GL5 2QG

Typesetting and origination by Tempus Publishing Ltd.
Printed and bound in Great Britain.

British Library Cataloguing in Publication Data.
A catalogue record for this book is available from the British Library.

ISBN 07524 1416 X

Contents

Historic Wreck Locations

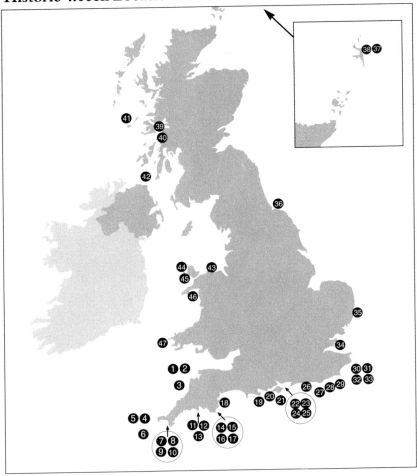

This book is dedicated to Alexander Flinder MBE who personifies the link between sport diving and archaeology underwater. A past Chairman of the British Sub-Aqua Club he was one of the founders of the Nautical Archaeology Society and served on the Advisory Committee on Historic Wreck Sites from its inception. His enthusiasm for archaeology is matched by a conviction that it is a source of enjoyment for all divers and a discipline to which they can contribute immeasurably. His writing, particularly the regular column for *Diver Magazine*, demystifies underwater archaeology. His approach has inspired us in writing this book. Its preparation has made us more aware of the amount of time, energy and money expended by sport divers in finding and investigating historic shipwrecks. It is a tribute to their commitment.

Preface

The world watched on televison as Henry VIII's flagship was raised from the seabed in 1982. It was placed alongside Nelson's *Victory* in Portsmouth Historic Dockyard. This signified her importance in Britain's maritime history and ensured that *Mary Rose* is a household name.

On the seabed her remains had been protected from accidental damage or wilful interference by designation under the Protection of Wrecks Act, passed nine years earlier in 1973. By 1998 forty-seven sites have been protected under the same Act. They have been investigated, for the most part, by enthusiastic sport divers devoting their spare time, applying their diverse skills and spending their own money on underwater archaeology. However, for the majority of people these shipwrecks are an unknown part of the UK's national heritage.

Designated Historic Wrecks in UK territorial waters span some three millennia of seaborne endeavour. They represent the vessels of nine countries. Merchantmen and naval ships, their losses touch many episodes of British history. They show the unique potential of wreck sites to illumine every century of the past, not only in terms of the international events of diplomacy, war and trade, but in the everyday lives of people: the utensils from their kitchens, the clothes they wore, the games they enjoyed and the instruments they played.

This book, published in the 25th year of the Protection of Wrecks Act, provides the first illustrated description of the forty-seven wrecks. The Introduction explains the stormy background which led to the Act. The shipwrecks are arranged in twelve chapters under broad themes which show their place in the development of ships and the history of trade and war at sea. For each wreck a description of the discovery and investigation shows the many challenges faced by divers applying archaeology underwater. The concluding analysis considers the shipwrecks as a national resource.

For twenty-five years the Act has conferred a measure of protection on a few wreck sites. Six months after it was passed the Under Secretary of State wrote:

> Its purpose is simply to ensure that designated wreck sites are protected from unauthorised interference and not ... to achieve the recovery and proper treatment for the public benefit of the cultural information represented by such objects.

There would be public outcry if this limited objective was applied to the best historical and archaeological monuments on land. The 1973 legislation is insufficient; for the UK the integration of land and seabed archaeology is overdue.

February 1998

Illustrations

Uncredited illustrations are the authors' own.

Colour Plates (between pages 64 and 65)

Cover Illustrations

Acknowledgements

Most of the shipwrecks described in this book have been found, researched and investigated by people working in their spare time. Without their efforts Britain's underwater archaeology would be poorly understood. Alison and Valerie are grateful to the many people who have patiently fielded questions and provided information and illustrations.

Jonathan Adams; Christian Ahlström; Stuart Bacon; Alan Bax; Lord Belhaven & Stenton; Jane & John Bingeman; Mike Bowyer; British Museum – Paul Craddock, Stuart Needham; Brunswick Developments (Sussex) Ltd – R Hagley; Chris Burls, Hydrographer Port of London Authority; Simon Burton; Toni Carrell, Ships of Discovery, Texas; Carl Olof Cederlund; Timothy Concannon; John Cross; Paul Dart; Peter Davies; Chris Dobbs; Richard Endsor; Environment & Heritage Service, Northern Ireland – Brian Williams; Alexander Flinder; Lady Aileen Fox; Jerzy Gawronski; Vincent Gillen; McClean Museum; Schip-Amsterdam; Mike Hall; John Heath; Historic Scotland – Noel Fojut; Matt Geen, Submetrix Ltd; Roy Graham; Hampshire & Wight Trust for Maritime Archaeology – Gary Momber; Islay Museum Trust; Keith Jarvis, Poole Museums Service; Lisberg Jensen; Cecil Jones; Richard Larn; Lundy Marine Nature Reserve; Colin JM Martin; Colin Martin, Joseph Sherburn Ltd; Mike Markey; Stan Merrals; Peter Moir; Peter Marsden; Mary Rose Trust – Alex Hildred; David Motkin; Michael Müller-Wille; National Maritime Museum – Geraldine Charles, Peter Van der Merwe; National Museums of Scotland; National Museum of Wales; Dave Perkins, Thanet Archaeological Unit; Ernest Perry; Brian Philp; Plymouth Underwater Archaeological Interest Group; Plymouth City Museum; Ray Pringle-Scott; Ramsgate Maritime Museum – Diane Chamberlain, Michael Hunt; Anthony Randall; Jeanette Ratcliffe, Cornwall Archaeology Unit; Receiver of Wreck – Veronica Robbins; RCAHMW – Gareth Edwards, RCHME – Steve Waring; Carole Rule; Nick Rule; Owain Roberts; Phil Robertson; Royal Armouries – Ruth Brown, Rob Smith; Royal Navy Submarine Museum; St Mary's Museum – Steve Ottery; Louise Sandeberg; Tim Sharpe; Rob Serrat; Robert Stenuit; South-West Maritime Archaeological Group, Neville Oldham, Mike Palmer, Mike Williams; Sutcliffe Gallery, Whitby; Ted Sutton; Matthew Tanner; Tees Archaeology – Garry Green; David Tomalin; Humphrey Wakefield; Tommy Watt, Shetland Museum; Sidney Wignall; Maurice Williams – Florida Museum of Natural History.

How to Use this Book

The forty-seven Historic Wrecks are described in twelve chapters. The individual entry for each shipwreck gives the name by which the wreck site is known, whether a ship name or a place name followed by the place and county.

Boxed details give the location and the area of seabed which is protected. HISTORICAL facts are quoted for wrecks of identifed ships. ARCHAEOLOGICAL data are given for unidentified wrecks and the entries are based on seabed observations alone.

Wreck Name
Location, County

General Location: National Grid Reference
Protection: latitude and longitude stated in the designation order and area protected.

INFORMATION SUMMARY

Built: year, place. Builder
Type: of ship eg paddle steamer, yacht
Dimensions: length x breadth in feet (metric conversion)
Armament: number of guns
Lost: day month year
Voyage: departure to destination
Cargo: summary of goods aboard
Complement: note of people aboard
Saved: note of survivors

Site Plan
A simplified plan indicates the extent or character of the site. Where a site plan was unavailable a location map or location photograph is given

Description of ship, loss, discovery and investigation of wreck site.
Viewpoint: indicates where the site may be viewed from the coast. When a site photograph is included the information appears within the caption.
Display: notes where artefacts from or information about the shipwreck are displayed or stored.
Further Reading: a book or article is given as a source of more information. For unpublished wrecks their entry is noted in the volumes, so far issued, of the *Shipwreck Index of the British Isles.* A list of general further reading appears on p153.

Finding A Historic Wreck

Geographical List (p7); Alphabetical list (p15); Chronological list (p146)

Measurements
Since the original ships were built to non-metric units these are given in text with metric conversions provided in brackets. The same convention is used for measurements recorded before metrication. For modern measurements the metric unit appears first with the imperial conversion in brackets. For general statements of depth or distance metres are used.

Alphabetical List of Historic Wrecks

Bold type indicates documented dates. Other dates are deduced from archaeological information, such as date-marked coins.

Ship	Built	Lost	Page
Admiral Gardner	1798	1809	80
Amsterdam	1742	1743	76
Anne	1678	1689	94
Assurance	1747	1753	131
Bartholomew Ledge	1555	1555	54
Brighton Marina	1500	1500	60
Cattewater	1530	1530	42
Church Rocks	1580	1580	66
Colossus	1787	1798	128
Coronation	1685	1690	102
Dartmouth	1655	1690	110
Duart Point	1640	1653	106
Dunwich Bank	1580	1580	68
Erme Estuary	1700	1700	58
Erme Ingot	1000	1000	30
Girona	1588	1588	64
Grace Dieu	1418	1439	36
Gull Rock	1500	1500	56
Hanover	1763	1763	114
Hazardous	1703	1706	134
Invincible	1744	1758	136
Iona II	1863	1864	140
Kennemerland	1661	1664	74
Langdon Bay	-1100	-1100	26
Mary	1660	1675	112
Mary Rose	1509	1545	38
Moor Sand	-1100	-1100	28
Northumberland	1679	1703	99
Pomone	1805	1811	131
Pwll Fanog	1575	1575	120
Restoration	1678	1703	101
Resurgam	1879	1880	143
Rhinns of Islay	1700	1700	70
Rill Cove	1603	1603	52
Royal Anne	1709	1721	90
Salcombe Cannon	1640	1640	86
Schiedam	1684	1684	84
Seaton Carew	1800	1800	118
Smalls	1060	1060	32
St Anthony	1527	1527	50
Stirling Castle	1678	1703	96
Studland Bay	1520	1520	44
S. Edinburgh Channel	1787	1787	78
Tal-y-Bont	1702	1702	122
Tearing Ledge	1678	1707	126
Wrangels Palais	1662	1687	88
Yarmouth Roads	1567	1567	46

Local people were trained as guides in readiness to welcome people aboard *Endeavour* during her call at Whitby. The crowds were infected with a carnival-like excitement.

Introduction

It is 7.30. In the grey morning light a small crowd stands beside Captain Cook's *Endeavour*, a copy which has already sailed half way round the world. As the sun rises the queue of couples and families, old and young, snakes along Whitby's quayside, over the bridge and into the town. In every port on her 1997 tour the scene was repeated. Patient crowds, thousands-strong, waited to walk aboard the 'real' ship recreated from documents. Everything excited curiosity and marvel; it was emotion not intellect as people reached back in wonder to the seamen who sailed her and the nation which sent her out across the world.

The legacy of centuries of seafaring is a wealth of truelife stories of disaster, tragedy and heroism. There is a charisma about ships both afloat, like the QE2 and the contestants in the Tall Ships Race, and lost, like *Lusitania* and Grace Darling's *Forfarshire*. Modern technology enables world-wide television audiences to experience deep-ocean spectacles such as salvage from the *Titanic*. There are many other shipwrecks whose discovery and investigation has not attracted the same level of media attention. Yet they are unlocking, sometimes in minute detail, the secrets of many centuries of history. This book describes all those which have merited protection for their historical, archaeological or artistic value.

Maritime Millennia

Television has made archaeology under water accessible to all. The coverage given when *Mary Rose* was raised introduced millions to the delights which awaited their personal visit to the Ship Hall and Exhibition in Portsmouth. While the scientific excavation of the hull has filled voids in knowledge of Tudor shipwrightry, the meticulous recovery and conservation of its contents enables anyone to appreciate the details of domestic and naval life under Henry VIII. This treasure trove of history was brought ashore with the help of hundreds of volunteer divers.

In every industrial port, small harbour and fishing cove there are reminders that Britain is a seafaring nation. These may be quayside warehouses, breakwaters, lighthouses, lifeboat stations or monuments to those lost at sea. Often a redundant maritime building now greets visitors as a museum. The coast is still a major tourist attraction, and heritage provides both entertainment and education.

In the UK the familiar brown of tourist signs will lead to the maritime museums, but they will not show the way to the seabed equivalent of prehistoric stone circles, medieval castles and industrial buildings. Just as historic sites can be protected by law so can shipwrecks. However, the law and the resources for land and sea are very different. The scheduled ancient monuments of the UK run into tens of thousands, the protected wrecks number fewer than fifty. Interpretation centres encourage visits and understanding of land-based heritage; protected wrecks are out of bounds and little publicised. This book describes the forty-seven Historic Wrecks and where to see recovered objects and the sites themselves. Most can be easily overlooked from promenades, seafront car parks and coastal paths. The drama of the shipwreck can be visualised in the same way that battlefields come alive when imagination and history combine.

The UK's shipwrecks are part of a wider maritime landscape. This can be appreciated from the panoramic viewpoint of an imaginary hilltop on the Atlantic edge of the European mainland. Far to the left, beyond the land barrier of the French Pyrenees, is the narrow Strait of Gibraltar separating Europe from Africa. To the right Denmark reaches across the mouth of the Baltic towards the incised coast of Norway, which stretches north into the Arctic Circle. Nestled in this sweep of coast is a North Sea archipelago strung out from the Shetland Isles in the north-east, only 200 miles (320km) from Norway, to the Isles of Scilly in the south-west, only 100 miles (160 km) from the French coast. Now called the British Isles, this offshore group has always been bound to the European continent by the narrow seas between.

The 3000-year-old boat described in chapter one is the earliest nautical evidence for the Channel crossing. However the distribution of artefacts in north-west Europe shows that the Atlantic seaways were used throughout prehistory. Roman writers recorded the goods received in Rome from Britain. Excavation of Anglo-Saxon and Viking settlements and cemeteries has made obvious the interaction with Scandinavia and the eastern Mediterranean. The arrival of a Norman ruling class only strengthened links across the narrow seas. The expanding populations of Europe exchanged their goods by river and sea. Britain was a part of this growing market. Her ports and anchorages received goods from, and provided shelter for, the ships of Europe's seafaring countries, from Venice to Russia.

Where Ships are Lost

The Historic Wrecks show some of the many causes of shipping accidents. Tempestuous weather might swamp a vessel; the Pwll Fanog slate wreck would have literally gone down like a stone. Often sinking was caused by decaying or damaged hulls letting in too much water for the crew to control with the pumps. *Iona II* was abandoned when too full of water to steer. Her crew made it to land, but similar circumstances could claim ships far from the sight of land leaving no survivors to record the event.

Ships faced greater risk of destruction when they came close to the coast. Here there were many hazards such as isolated rocks and submerged reefs. In the bad visibility of gale and fog *Kennemerland* and *Wrangels Palais* hit outliers of the Shetlands, and the Smalls Reef, Pembrokeshire, probably claimed a Viking ship. The land itself was a hazard. In the English Channel the west-facing coasts of the Lizard, Start Point and the Isle of Wight were all key obstacles. In south-westerly winds ships drove onto these lee shores if the master was not sure of his position, or, through force of weather or failure of equipment, he could not tack to clear the headlands. This was the fate of *Schiedam* and probably of the ship in Rill Cove nearby.

Poor navigation was a great problem. The sounding lead was essential. The most experienced seamen came to grief because they lacked good navigational instruments. Measuring latitude required clear weather to see sun or stars and there was no readily available instrument for measuring longitude until the late eighteenth century. Admiral Clowdisley Shovell's fleet thought themselves far south of the Isles of Scilly when Tearing Ledge took one of their ships, three others being lost on nearby reefs.

When it was clear that a ship would not survive a captain often tried to run it onto an open beach in the hope of saving crew and cargo. The *Amsterdam* made it onto the beach. If the captain of *St Anthony* tried the same manoeuvre he was unlucky in striking a reef just offshore, a situation mirrored at Church Rocks and Tal-y-Bont.

Entering anchorages and harbour was a particularly dangerous time. Ships needed the know-how of local pilots to negotiate narrow or twisting channels. Masters aboard *Assurance* and *Pomone* misjudged the western entrance to the Solent. *Hazardous* found herself on shoals and a lee shore as she tried to come into the Solent anchorages from the east. Precise shiphandling was needed to carry a ship clear and, a result of first her anchor and then her steering gear jamming, *Invincible* grounded on sand banks while trying to leave St Helens Road.

Even at anchor ships were not safe. *Swan*, *Dartmouth* and *Colossus* were torn from their anchors by violent storms and driven onto rocks, while *Restoration*, *Northumberland*, *Stirling Castle* and *Admiral Gardner* were similarly driven from the safety of the Downs onto the shifting Goodwin Sands.

There were losses during battles. If the Dunwich Bank Wreck had proved to be the hoped-for *Royal James* it would be a true battle casualty. More often losses were only indirectly caused by the enemy. Thus *Mary Rose* sank because her gunports allowed water in and *Anne* was run ashore to prevent her being captured.

Finally, some 'wrecks' were not lost by accident. The redundant *Grace Dieu* was laid up and the ship at Seaton Carew may have been run onto the beach for the same reason.

How Shipwrecks are Found

Some wrecks have always been known. Around the muddy fringes of harbours and rivers are the decaying remains of boats and ships which were left to rot where they lay. Vessels which sank to the seabed are more difficult to locate and identify.

There are many records of ship losses. Records were usually made because the ship was of economic importance. A foreign merchant, for example, in dispute with salvors might petition the King. Resulting correspondence may survive in the Calendars of State Papers. Petitions are also preserved in the High Court of Admiralty papers. Local landowners often had the right to claim wreck. Their letters might include a note of money received for recovered cargo or salvaged parts of hulls. These economic worries tell little of the actual ships and their position. Yet such records are the only source of information for many merchant ships lost before the eighteenth century.

Naval courts martial, on the other hand, focus on the wreck event. The questioning officers, like modern accident investigators, wanted to know why the ship was lost and would pursue information on her course, the weather, her condition and the actions of officers and crew. As *Coronation* and *Colossus* show, courts martial, coupled with ships' logs, can be used very accurately to reconstruct the events and location of naval vessels lost from the late seventeenth century onwards.

In contrast a note of a merchant ship loss can be very brief, such as the perfunctory news in *Lloyd's List*, a shipping paper published twice weekly from 1746. Local newspapers and the diaries of local people can flesh out the story. Remote communities have long memories passed in story form. For both *Kennemerland* and *Dartmouth* locally-told tales of the wrecking still survive and match the discoveries made by archaeologists.

Sometimes the name of the ship passes into local language, giving its name to a place; *Hanover* was discovered in Hanover Cove. Occasionally the moment of shipwreck was captured by an artist. Paintings always raise questions of accuracy versus artistic licence but that of *Pomone* striking the Needles fits very well with naval accounts and the seabed archaeology. Charts can be more helpful, although divers argue over whether Gostelo was mistaken in marking *Romney* on Tearing Ledge on his contemporary map of the Isles of Scilly.

From the 1950s SCUBA gave the freedom for sport divers to explore the seabed and numerous wreck sites were discovered by chance. Historical records sometimes enabled them to identify the ships they found. Other divers set out to find a particular wreck after using every written record, map, illustration or folk-story to track down the details of its history and loss. This information then guided their search of the seabed.

Remote sensing surveys can cover large areas and pinpoint targets for divers to investigate. Magnetometers were among the first instruments commonly employed in wreck hunting. They measure changes in magnetic resistivity and so are able to locate objects such as iron guns and ballast either on or in the seabed. In the late 1960s Alex Mckee used the best available remote sensing equipment to narrow the search for the *Mary Rose*.

Surveys locate wrecks because they appear as anomalies on the strip of seabed being mapped. Sophisticated surveys combine several instruments. In principle they all work by emitting a signal which is reflected back from the seabed; the time-lapse is measured and converted into a visual image. Echo sounders and sidescan sonars measure the distance to the seabed. The first projects a simple downward signal and so only gives depth, while the latter sends signals in an oblique pattern and records the changing surface of a swathe of seabed, thus identifying any wreck which is on, or protruding from, it. Sub-bottom profilers send a signal which penetrates the seabed and records changes in the material beneath. They can locate buried wreckage.

Using a metal-detector to probe the kelp forest on the Kennemerland *site. On many sites investigation begins with the task of clearing the kelp, cutting each stalk by hand. Weed cover is one of the many problems to consider when selecting wreck sites for diver trails.*

Position fixing is essential to good survey. A boat and divers must be able to return to the same spot. The search for the *Coronation* took so many years that position fixing progressed from the use of manual transits and sextant readings to electronic positioning using decca. Now global positioning systems (GPS) use satellites to achieve very great accuracy.

For early remote sensing instruments the output was literally a long paper trace of the seabed. It was difficult to correlate the information from different instruments deployed during a survey. With ever-increasing computer technology the output is now recorded digitally. This means that it can be interrogated and manipulated with greater speed and flexibility. The output from each instrument is fitted like a mosaic into a single 'picture'. The final paper product can be a sophisticated 3-D image of the data from every component in the survey. Survey systems used over *Resurgam* are so accurate that small objects could be located to within half a metre, while on the *Assurance/Pomone* site the fissured rock formation of the seabed has been mapped right to the water's edge with the precision of 20cm (8in) contours.

The high-tech approach to wreck-hunting has a second dimension. Remotely operated vehicles (ROV) can carry videos and infra-red cameras which see better than man and their robotic arms can be used to recover objects.

The Cost of Salvage

There is no longer any part of UK territorial seas which is beyond the capability of modern salvage techniques. Commercial salvors target cargo whose sale exceeds the cost of recovery. It is not only recent shipwrecks whose contents can attract investors for salvage expeditions. Some objects such as raw metals have intrinsic value regardless of age. Antiques have a retail value. This can be inflated when the contents of a ship are auctioned. A simple wooden platter can fetch over £800. Publicity plays on the public fascination with seafaring, disasters and recovered 'treasure'. Museums bid alongside the public.

Commercial salvage aims to bring items to the surface as efficiently as possible to maximise the return on sale, whereas recovery is only a tool of archaeological investigation and not its prime objective. Archaeological study of a wreck aims to record the maximum information about a wreck site in order to discover as much as possible about the original ship, its builders, sailors, cargo and the communities which it served. Vital information is collected by recording objects and their location. There is only one opportunity for this recording as the process of recovery destroys the seabed site.

Clearly salvage techniques can be too destructive for archaeological purposes; and archaeological techniques too slow for the economics of commercial salvage. Differences between archaeological and commercial practice go deeper still. Excavation is only a small proportion of an archaeological project. Post-excavation tasks include meticulous drawing, photographing, scientific analysis and historical research into every recovered object. The aim is comprehensive publication to make the information from the site available to others. This can require keeping the excavated objects together for years. Where storage facilities permit, the objects and associated records ideally remain together as a resource for future research.

Salvage is a legitimate activity, recovering a seabed resource in the same way as other operations extract commodities such as gravel or oil. It is now widely understood that winning the resources of land and sea often has a cost measured as a loss or deterioration of the natural and human heritage. The heritage is only safeguarded if development activity is regulated voluntarily or by statute. As archaeologists and salvors explore the boundaries of underwater technology it is vital that they discover working methods that ensure a balance between commercial exploitation and heritage preservation.

Twenty-Five Years of Historic Wreck Protection

The aqualung placed the seabed in reach of increasing numbers of divers. Treasure was no longer a dream. Anyone was at liberty to recover objects by any means from the UK seabed provided they were then declared to the Receiver of Wreck and their disposal was handled in accordance with Merchant Shipping Law. However, in the UK and other countries the increased stripping of wreck sites was also seen as piecemeal and irreversible destruction of the maritime heritage. Governments reacted with protective legislation. In some countries this took the form of blanket protection of all wrecks over a certain age. The salvage lobby in the UK resisted any restriction on their activities. In 1970 a parliamentary move for a change in legislation had to be dropped. Uncontrolled salvage from historic wrecks went from bad to worse with several suffering the depredations of rival teams of divers. Finally, in 1973, a Private Member's bill was successfully steered through parliament.

The Protection of Wrecks Act (1973) allows designation of a restricted area around the seabed site of a vessel on account of the historical, archaeological or artistic importance of the vessel, its contents or former contents. It applies in UK waters excluding the Isle of Man and the Channel Islands. It is an offence for unauthorised persons to tamper with, damage or remove any part of the wreck or its contents; to carry out diving or salvage operations; and to deposit anything which would obliterate or obstruct access to the site. Activity can only be undertaken under licence. There have been two types of licence. A survey licence allows the applicant and other named individuals to undertake survey and other similar non-destructive work within the designated area. An excavation licence must be obtained before anything is raised from a Historic Wreck. Two new categories have been added: visitor licences for sites where there is no active work; survey recovery licences to recover exposed material.

Responsibility for the Act has been passed, like an unwanted child, from the Department of Trade and Industry to the Department of Transport, to the Department of the Environment and then to the Department of National Heritage, now Culture, Media and Sport. In Northern Irish, Scottish and Welsh waters authority is respectively vested in the Department of the Environment Northern Ireland and the Secretaries of State for Scotland and Wales.

The Advisory Committee on Historic Wreck Sites (ACHWS) advises the Secretary of State on designations and licences. As a result of lobbying by the Council for British Archaeology and the Nautical Archaeology Society, the Department of Transport in 1986 agreed to make available funds to contract a field team to support the ACHWS. Before that time the Advisory Committee Members had perforce to visit ('inspect') sites themselves. The contract was awarded to the University of St Andrews which set up the Archaeological Diving Unit (ADU). It was charged with visiting designated sites and those proposed for designation. The main aims of the ADU are now: to ascertain the extent of work undertaken by licensees; to discuss working methods with them; to observe standards of work and compliance with licence conditions; to provide general advice and assistance if required; and to provide for the Department for Culture, Media and Sport a report on each site visit.

The Act has not lived up to expectations. Protection from interference is its stated purpose. Responsibility falls to local police forces but no resources are made available for this task. The option of emergency designation has not been used to provide temporary designation when a site is first reported. This would control activity until sufficient information has been gathered for a decison on further designation to be made.

On land archaeological sites are no longer treated in isolation. Decisions over their protection and care are made with consideration both to set criteria and to the total of known sites, locally, regionally and nationally. In contrast wreck designation remains reactive rather than proactive and 'No rigid criteria have been defined for assessing wrecks for designation and decisions are made in the light of individual circumstances'.

The bulk of expenditure in respect of the Act is on the contract with the Archaeological Diving Unit. The Act conferred no funding for survey, excavation, conservation and publication of designated wrecks. Few sites have been provided with interpretation panels. The lack of marker buoys has been a cause of complaint.

The Future

The majority of older wrecks were discovered and investigated by sport and salvage divers. Once the new Act imposed archaeological constraints, however minimal, it was clear that a nationwide elementary training programme in techniques of survey, excavation and first-aid conservation was desperately overdue.

The Nautical Archaeology Society took up the challenge. It built on the pioneer training programmes of Fort Bovisand and the Council for Nautical Archaeology and developed a highly successful certification scheme. This has received government funding. Large numbers of divers have completed the basic training and have gone on to develop their archaeological skills under water. Despite a lack of career opportunities in the UK maritime archaeological options at university level are increasingly popular. As a result there is now a significant number of divers with the skills and interest to take an active part in maritime archaeology.

Access to Historic Wrecks has been limited to divers named under the licensing procedure. This has recently been re-interpreted to allow the licensees to invite visits from the public on specific days. Underwater parks in other countries show that visiting divers can be given much freer access to historic shipwrecks. Here in the UK assessment of shipwrecks in Marine Nature Reserves suggests that there are many where divers' enjoyment and safety could be enhanced by some form of management and interpretation.

Ideally the total shipwreck resource of the UK should be considered in decision-making. Appropriate judgements could then be made regarding: which receive protection to exclude divers; which require resources for rescue or research excavation; which are appropriate for interpretation to encourage visits; which should be left as wildlife habitats; and which are suitable for salvage. Such decisions require information on every located wreck site, a data-gathering task beyond present, and even dreamt of, archaeological funding. Only sport divers can provide the information. A form *Dive into History* enables divers to report their observations of wrecks for entry in national registers of underwater sites maintained nationally in England, Scotland, Wales and Northern Ireland. As many as 1.5 million dives in UK waters were logged in 1997. Underwater archaeology is one point where culture and sport can meet.

1 Untold Voyages

Famous disasters at sea are part of living history. Ship names – *Titanic, Torrey Canyon, Herald of Free Enterprise* – instantly conjure up images. In contrast the four oldest wreck sites in UK waters have no ship names and no written history. Their existence and fate is known only from objects found on the seabed in the last twenty years. Yet they open our eyes to more than 3000 years of sea voyages and trade.

On none of these early sites is there any trace of the ship itself, merely the metalwork which they were carrying. To gain an idea of the vessels, the remains of ships found elsewhere, or contemporary pictures, need to be used.

Langdon Bay (see Colour Plate 1)
Dover, Kent

General Location: TR 3414 4176
Protection: 51° 07.60'N 01° 20.80'E, 150m radius

ARCHAEOLOGICAL

Lost: 12th century BC
Cargo: bronze tools as scrap metal

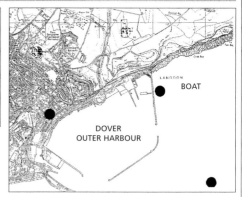

Map of Dover Harbour to show the location of the Bronze Age boat (left) and the Langdon Bay bronzes (right).

The accessibility and slack water of Langdon Bay just to the east of Dover Harbour, make it a popular dive site for Dover Sub Aqua Club. During a routine dive in August 1974 Mike Hadlow and Simon Stevens spotted some small metal objects which were quite different from the usual World War ll debris lying on the fissured chalk. Having recovered a spearhead and five other items they visited the curator of Dover Museum. The objects were instantly recognised as Bronze Age weapons and tools more than 3000 years old, and advice was sought from Brian Philp and the Kent Archaeological Rescue Unit.

Over the next two years members of Dover SAC recovered about 90 bronzes from a depth of 7-13m. Nothing comparable was known from land sites and in 1979 the British Museum, National Maritime Museum and British Sub Aqua Club sponsored a full season of work. Guided by Keith Muckelroy, Dover SAC excavated a 15m long trench and carried out an intensive surface search mapping the location of every find. Work on the site has continued and the total number is now 363. They date to the end of the Middle Bronze Age, around 1150BC. There has been some suggestion that the bronzes had eroded out of the cliff and had not come from a shipwreck. However, their sheer quantity as well as their foreign manufacture, their concentration in a radius of some 50m and their location 500m from the shore (even allowing for erosion) all show that this was cargo from a shipwreck and not just objects which had fallen from the cliffs above.

The bronzes are very worn as a result of exposure on the seabed for some time. They appear to have been cut up as scrap metal. There are three kinds of axe, a large number of rapier blades, spearheads, pins and a knife blade – plus bracelet fragments. Their shape betrays their European origin. For instance, the spearheads have holes for fixing hafts by means of pegs, whereas British spears were fastened to their shafts by means of loops. The only obviously British tool is a socketed axe – perhaps this belonged to the ship and was not part of the cargo.

It seems that the bronzes had been assembled from a wide area on the Continent and were being brought to Britain for melting down. We can only guess what goods they would have been exchanged for. The importance of wreck deposits to land archaeologists is made clear from just one fact: at least 50 'median winged axes' were in the cargo. This far exceeds even the largest European hoard, from Longueville in France, which had just six examples.

For prehistoric man his axe was his chief tool and wood his chief material. Improved ways of fixing a bronze axe to its haft were found. The 'winged palstave' was a Continental development and identifed the Langdon Bay bronzes as imports.

Simple flat axe   'Palstave'   'Winged palstave'   Socketed axe with loop
(Bindings are omitted for clarity)

Many archaeologists had dismissed underwater exploration as too ship-orientated and more relevant to modern periods. The Langdon Bay wreck site has turned distribution maps upside down and shown every prehistorian that underwater discoveries can revolutionise understanding of trade and society.

The Missing Ship

Bronze Age rock carvings in Scandinavia showed ships with large crews. A chance discovery in Dover has given substance to these images

of prehistoric seafaring. A superb plank boat was found, beneath 7m of accumulated soil, in the prehistoric inlet. Its massive oak planks, intricately carved and fitted, showed how ships as much as 15m long were in use in the second millennium BC. No metal, wooden pegs or ribs were used in its construction, and it had no keel. Instead 'stitches', each one made from a thin yew branch twisted to make it pliable, fastened the planks together and wedges secured the central seam. Layers of moss waterproofed the seams and were fixed in position by battens beneath the stitches. In order to understand the

technology a full-sized section of the boat was built using copies of Bronze Age tools fitted with a variety of hafts. Much has incidentally been learned about the efficiency of the tools for working unseasoned oak timber. The perfectly preserved tool-marks and fine woodworking of the original have been faithfully copied and give an idea of the quality of prehistoric houses, furniture and waggons.

Viewpoint: car parks on the cliffs above Dover Ferry Port
Display: Dover Museum; Collection: British Museum
Further reading: Muckelroy, K. 1981. Middle Bronze Age trade between Britain and Europe. *Proceedings of the Prehistoric Society, 47: 275-97*

Moor Sand (see Colour Plate 1; page 151)
Prawle, Point Devon

General Location: SX 7595 3615
Protection: 50° 12.70'N   03° 44.33'W,   300m
radius.

ARCHAEOLOGICAL

Lost: 12th century BC
Cargo: bronze weapons as scrap metal

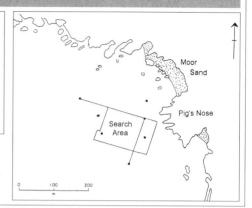

After sport divers found seven bronzes the National Maritime Museum led a seabed survey. The plan shows the searched area

It is fitting that the site of a prehistoric shipwreck should have been found on a beautiful stretch of Devon's coastline which remains untouched by modern activity. Prawle Point is in the care of the National Trust and a coastal path leads westwards to the little cove of Moor Sand where a battered government notice gives no hint of the excitement of a discovery made in 1977.

The clear water and gently shelving beach made Moor Sand an ideal spot for Philip Baker to give his class of YHA holidaymakers an unforgettable dive. This is what it proved to be for him also. In shallow water between two large rocks he saw a sword blade lying on the gravel bottom. Then shortly afterwards one of the novice divers found another one also lying on the seabed 5 - 6m below. Philip Baker happened to have an interest in swords and immediately recognised the importance of the finds. As he lived in Doncaster it was

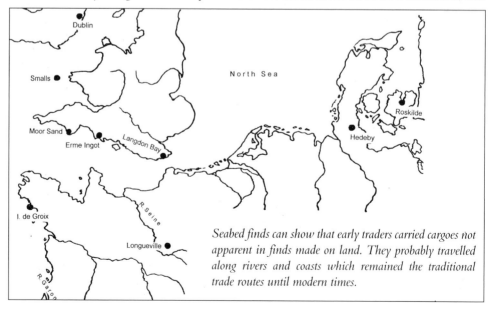

Seabed finds can show that early traders carried cargoes not apparent in finds made on land. They probably travelled along rivers and coasts which remained the traditional trade routes until modern times.

the museum there which he approached and which undertook to conserve them. The possibility that these Bronze Age weapons had come from a shipwreck more than 3000 years old was of national interest. Five more bronzes were found, two of which were axes (palstaves) in deeper water 100m seaward of the other finds. Application for designation of an area 600m in diameter was successful and the British Museum, British Academy and National Maritime Museum sponsored further investigations on the site.

This enabled a major search to be undertaken in 1979. Over four weeks a team of 13 divers with metal-detecting equipment failed to find any more artefacts or evidence of a shipwreck. The last artefact to come from the site was a badly worn rapier or sword recovered from the shallows near where the first discovery was made.

The question was how the bronzes came to be in the sea. The biggest argument for a shipwreck was that the swords and axes belonged to the same period of the Middle Bronze Age – about the twelfth century BC – and were not made in Britain but must have crossed the sea. The first find, Philip Baker's sword, was made from a low tin alloy, had shallow grooves on its shoulder, plus a blade and tang cross-section like 'Urnfield' swords which are found on the Continent from southern Germany to west of the River Seine. The two axes are of a design commonly found in Britanny and have led to the hypothesis that this was a cargo being brought not via the Dover Straits but by the longer sea route from north-west France to the West Country.

Viewpoint: Looking from the shelving shingle beach of Moor Sand to Pig's Nose. Bronze swords found in the shallow water show that a boat probably overturned here in the twelfth century BC. The South West Coast Path leads past Pig's Nose and a steep path leads to the Sand.

Collection: British Museum
Further reading: Muckelroy, K. 1980. Two Bronze Age cargoes in British waters. *Antiquity*, 54: 100-9; see also Langdon Bay

Erme Ingot
Erme Estuary, Devon

General Location: SX 6066 4663
Protection: 50° 18.15′N 03° 57.41′W, 100m radius

ARCHAEOLOGICAL

Lost: uncertain
Cargo: tin ingots

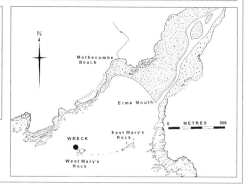

Throughout prehistory and up to modern times the mining of metals has stimulated seaborne trade and communications. The transport of New World and African gold, Spanish and Portuguese silver, Swedish copper and British lead appears in later chapters. A scatter of tin ingots beside a reef in a small river mouth has provided unique early evidence for the West Country's trade in a metal which was needed to make copper into a harder and more useful material.

In 1992 a scatter of 44 ingots was found in the Erme Estuary by divers from the South-West Maritime Archaeological Group. They lay on the landward side of West Mary's Rocks, among loose rocks, sand and kelp at a depth of 7-10m. The Group were already working close by on a designated wreck site. They recognised the importance of having these mysterious and unglamorous objects identified and were able to set about gridding the reef in order to plot the position of each ingot. More detailed investigation is no longer easy as sand has built up over the site.

The divers would not have spotted the ingots without metal detectors and most would not have given them a second look. They ranged in size from a fist to a rugby ball; the tin had blistered, producing nodules and scars; accretions of shells and worm casts covered them; and the sea had done its worst to abrade and corrode them. The ingots as recovered weighed 84.6kg (186lb), equivalent to a man. The forms included round and oval buns and little 'H' shapes.

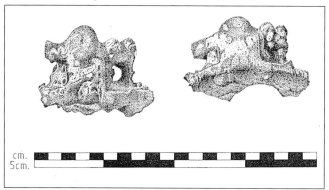

cm.
5cm.

Part-time archaeologists bring a wide range of skills to the study of the wreck sites. This meticulous drawing of the knarled surface of two of the ingots was made by Rob Whale, an artist and member of the team.

Even on land sites tin ingots are very rare. Consequently the new finds could not be dated, but their range of shapes and weights suggested that they were made by independent miners working on a small scale in an era before any standardisation was imposed. The earliest tin workers could use the ore cassiterite which occurs in shallow alluvial deposits in the rivers of Devon and Cornwall, including the Erme. As yet no remains of prehistoric or early historic ore-working have been found on Dartmoor, but in Late Bronze Age huts on Dean Moor excavators found a cassiterite pebble and the by-product of smelting, namely, tin slag.

The tin deposits of Britain were noted by early explorers from the Mediterranean such as Pytheas in the fourth century BC. The tin was carried by ship across the Channel and then overland probably via the River Garonne and the Carcassonne Gap to the mouth of the Rhône. The British ingots are described as knuckle-shaped and it is possible that these were like the two 'H-shaped' ingots among the Erme examples. The Roman occupation of Britain disrupted this trade, but from the third century AD it clearly resumed. Bun-shaped ingots have come from a number of sites in the Isles of Scilly and Cornwall which are dated to the late Roman and early medieval periods. The earliest Christian converts in western Britain needed wine for the Eucharist, and fragments of the amphoras in which it was transported have been found on numerous sites. These include Mothecombe Beach close to the reef and Bantham, about 2km (1 mile) distant, which lends weight to the theory that tin ingots were being traded for wine in Bigbury Bay.

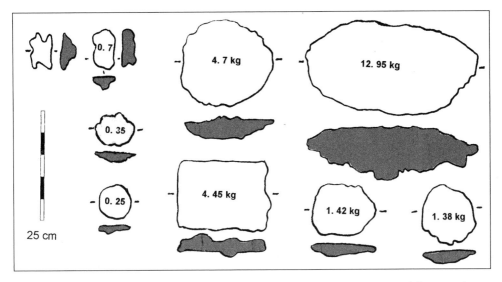

Industrialisation brings regulation and uniform products. In contrast the mixture of shapes and sizes shows these tin ingots were made by individual smelters, who probably combined their metal production with the seasonal tasks of farming. The tiniest ingots are H-shaped weighing only 260g.

Viewpoint: the South West Coast Path on the east side of the estuary. At low tide the sand bar can be seen across the river mouth and white water over West Mary's Rock
Display: Royal Albert Museum, Exeter
Further reading: Fox, A. 1995. Tin ingots from Bigbury Bay, South Devon. *Devon Archaeological Society Proceedings*, 53: 11-23

The Smalls
Smalls Reef, Dyfed

General Location: SM 4644 0876
Protection: 51° 43.18'N 05° 40.29'W, 100m radius

ARCHAEOLOGICAL

Lost: 11th century
Complement: possibly with a warrior chieftain

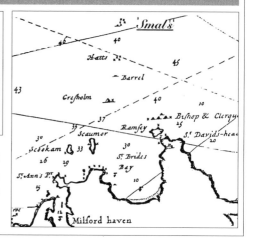

The Smalls is a navigational hazard recorded in the oldest sailing instructions. It lay on a sea route between Dublin and Denmark in the Viking era.

'The most beautiful dive site in Britain' was how a BSAC instructor described the Smalls. He could also have mentioned its remoteness, 25km (15 miles) out in the Irish Sea from the Pembrokeshire coast. Yet this is where, in August 1991, on an expedition with seven other divers from Milton Keynes SAC, Karen Anyon was diving in 15m-plus visibility on a site where modern ships have come to grief. Portions of steel plates littered the seabed. She noticed a bluish object protruding from beneath one of the plates which she thought at first was a fish. It proved to be a Viking sword guard of the most elaborate kind; its corroding silver inlays had caused the blue tint which caught her attention. Nothing else was found then or later and the puzzle remained as to how it had got there.

The Smalls was described in a seventeenth-century British pilot book as 'a small Rock always above the Water, about the bigness of a Long-Boat, and lieth to the Westward of Gresholm 2 Leagues and a half, or 3 Leagues. The West North West and North West end is foul and rocky a Mile off, and is deep too. The Tides run very strong amongst these Islands and Rocks.' This description is accompanied by charts of the entire coast, the result of a seven-year survey. Earlier seamen navigated these waters relying on information passed from generation to generation. A hint of their first-hand knowledge is preserved in a rare medieval manual: the 'sea goth half tide betwne the smale [Smalls] and Skidwhalles [St Tudwal's] and the bersays [Bardsey]. And it floweth est and west on the mayne londe and at the ramseir north and south the stremys renne in the sonde and be owten the Bishoppis and his clerkis north northwest and south south est ...' This text must echo the oral information which Viking Age seamen relied on.

Excavations in Dublin have shown the port was a great trading centre at this time. While Norsemen sailed round the north of Scotland to reach the Western Isles and Irish Sea, for the Danes the southern route was shorter. The Smalls was a hazard on the sea route between Denmark and Dublin. Proof that ships passed between Ireland and Denmark has been found in Roskilde. Scientists have now matched the pattern of tree rings from the waterlogged clinker planks of a ship, recovered in the 1960s, with the pattern of the growth of oaks from Ireland. This proves that the warship was built in Ireland from trees felled about AD 1060.

Unfortunately it was found empty of gear, very damaged and deliberately scuttled. It has a reconstructed length of 29.3m (96ft) with a height of only 1.8m (6ft). It would have had a crew of 60 oarsmen. Compared with the shorter, broader merchant ships found in the same fjord the warship is a true Viking longship.

Highly decorated swords were status symbols. For a warrior, burial in his longship with his sword was the ultimate memorial. Fine swords have been found buried in longships: at Hedeby, a prosperous Danish port, in a ship 30.9m (101ft) long; and on the Atlantic-swept Isle de Groix off the Britanny coast (Map p.28). Both date to the tenth century, a century earlier than the chieftain's sword lost on the Smalls.

Whether the travelling chieftain lost his sword overboard or went down with his ship only further investigation could show. The National Museum of Wales, which had acquired the guard, investigated the site but found no further trace of a ship. Initially an area 600m in diameter round the find spot was put out of bounds to divers. This effectively ruled out all diving on the popular Smalls, as *Diver Magazine* commented when the ban was challenged. In 1995 the restricted area was reduced to 200m diameter.

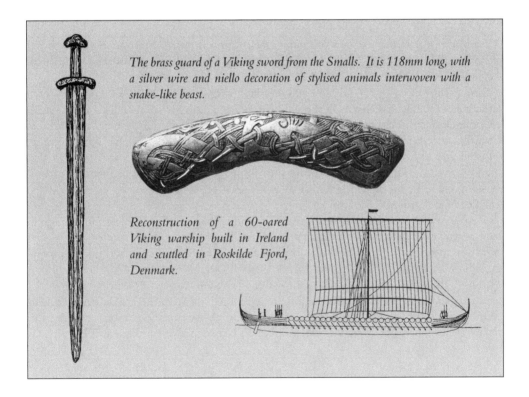

The brass guard of a Viking sword from the Smalls. It is 118mm long, with a silver wire and niello decoration of stylised animals interwoven with a snake-like beast.

Reconstruction of a 60-oared Viking warship built in Ireland and scuttled in Roskilde Fjord, Denmark.

Viewpoint: the Smalls lie 25km (15 miles) offshore
Collection: National Maritime Museum of Wales
Further reading: Redknap, M. 1992. A remarkable Viking find in a remote site. *Amgueddfa*, 14:9

What Makes a Wreck?

The Moor Sand and Langdon Bay searches began with discoveries of one or two bronze tools or weapons. When in 1991 Terry Cocker found a Bronze Age sword at Sennen Cove in Cornwall it did not spark the same response. Many bronze tools have been brought up in fishermen's nets, but it is difficult to pinpoint a findspot from the track of a trawl net.

Since the 1720s Roman pottery has been brought up in oystermen's trawls off Whitstable. The site is referred to as the Pudding Pan Wreck but has never been precisely located. Individual amphoras or fragments have also been trawled up from many places. Repeated finds in Yarmouth Roads, Isle of Wight, prompted an archaeological search of the location but no wreck was found.

The Smalls Historic Wreck Site is founded on the discovery of a single artefact. It is not the only Viking object recovered by divers. In 1981, for example, Martin Brown found a gold arm ring near Ruadh Sgeir in the Sound of Jura. This 'was not an area of inundated land; it had clearly arrived at its findspot during a sea crossing.' There were no resources to investigate the discovery and the site was not protected.

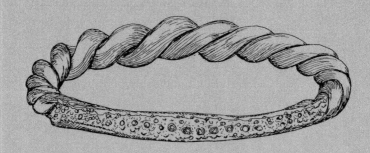

When a seabed find is reported to County Archaeologists or to the Royal Commission on Historic Monuments it will be entered into the records of archaeological sites. At present, it is unlikely to initiate a field search for a wreck site. This is understandable as single objects may arrive on the seabed by a variety of routes. However, with increasingly powerful remote sensing equipment it is feasible to search large areas of seabed for wreck sites. The accumulated data on seabed finds can be used to target these searches to areas where there is a greater probability of finding the medieval, Viking, Saxon, Roman and prehistoric wrecks which are needed to fill large gaps in our knowledge of seafaring around Britain.

2 The Kings' Ships

Two royal warships show the great contrast in what can survive for archaeological study. *Grace Dieu* is the bottom of an empty hulk. *Mary Rose* is a storehouse crammed with equipment and personal possessions. Historically each was among the greatest ships of its day: *Grace Dieu* built by order of Henry V and *Mary Rose* by Henry VIII. Their building, active service and fates are well-documented. The remains of both ships were discovered in the nineteenth century, surprisingly close to where each had been built. They were treated as antiquarian novelties. In this century they have been scientifically investigated. While the exceptional contents of *Mary Rose* have provided one of the country's most popular windows on Tudor life, *Grace Dieu* has remained obscure, except to those with a particular interest in ship construction.

Grace Dieu (see Colour Plate 2)
River Hamble, Hampshire

General Location: SU 5016 0687	
Protection: 50° 51′ 31″N 01° 17′ 14″W, 75m radius	
HISTORICAL	
Built: 1418, Southampton. William Soper	
Type: 'Great shippe'; carrack	
Dimensions: 175ft (53.3m)	
Lost: 1439, burnt while laid up in mud dock at Bursledon	

The existence of a great wooden wreck in the River Hamble seems always to have been known. On the lowest tides its overlapping planks showed above the river mud. Without the insight of ship archaeology the Victorians saw the clinker planking as proof it was a Viking wreck. However, it is now known to be the much later *Grace Dieu* laid down in 1416. Two things are remarkable about the ship: the way she is constructed and the detailed records left by her builder. Two hundred years would pass before a larger ship was built, and by then shipbuilders had opted for a different way of building ships.

Enthusiasm for practical nautical research was fostered, in the 1930s, by the Society for Nautical Research (SNR) which encouraged its members to record traditional boats. The Director of the Science Museum visited the wreck and challenged its Viking identity. The puzzle was taken up by three SNR members, Anderson, Naish and Prynne. The wreck is not easy to reach, and is only visible for an hour at the bottom of the lowest spring tides. Undeterred they completed a basic survey during 1933.

Their observations were dramatic. Each strake was a sandwich of three layers of clinker planking fastened with long nails and caulked with moss and tar. Treenails about $1\frac{1}{2}$ in (38mm) in diameter fastened the planking to close-set frames. The keel was found to be at least 127ft (38.7m) long and the remains suggested a beam in the region of 50ft (15.2m). An Elizabethan formula, the earliest known tonnage rule, was used to compute a size of 1400-1500 tons. The hull was extraordinary. The planking was counter to historical evidence for the construction of large ships which from the sixteenth century onwards were known to be built with carvel planking fastened to a pre-erected framework of keel and ribs.

In 1934 Anderson matched his mud-based observations with historical facts. 'The conclusion is so obvious that one almost hesitates to adopt it. The *Grace Dieu* of Henry V fits the bill exactly.' Once her identity was known her construction could be explained. When she was launched she was the largest ship ever built in northern Europe. She was a two-masted carrack with tall fighting castles fore and aft. To give her planking sufficient strength her builders hit on the idea of constructing it in three layers.

Although no painting of the ship has survived, contemporary manuscripts written in neat handwriting give a detailed picture of her and of medieval shipyard operations. She was part of a programme of warship construction directed by William Soper and funded directly by the King. Everything was recorded: building a 'dok' enclosed by a hedge of

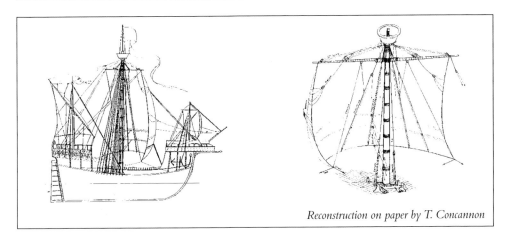

Reconstruction on paper by T. Concannon

spines and stakes; tradesmen and their wages; the stores, their costs and any amount recouped by later sale; ready-made naval gear and stores brought from captured ships; and the names of ships broken up locally for spare materials. Local forests also provided timber; with no fewer than 2610 oaks and 1165 beeches from the New Forest, and 'gifts' of timber from local monasteries.

The 'Great Shippe' was blessed in July 1418 and William Payne was commissioned her master in December. Only one sailing is documented, in 1420. It was a dismal failure with a mutinous crew. She was taken into Southampton Water and remained on a mooring for twelve years, manned by a skeleton crew. There she was something of a tourist attraction. An Italian visitor estimated the height of her forecastle and the size of her mainmast. The metric equivalents of the Italian bracchia are 16m above the waterline, 2m diameter at the upper deck and 60m high. He thought she was the most beautiful construction he had ever seen. Shortly afterwards, on a high tide, she was towed up the Hamble to a fenced mud berth. The end came when she was struck by lightning in 1439.

As a commissioned ship she remained government property until 1970 when Southampton University purchased her from the Ministry of Defence for £5. Three years later the site was one of the first to be designated under the Protection of Wrecks Act. From 1980 to 1983 an archaeological survey and assessment of the site was undertaken by the, now defunct, Archaeological Research Centre of the National Maritime Museum. The hull was found to survive to a height of only a metre or so.

The value of these hull remains is unquestionable. They are the only known example of composite clinker construction. *Grace Dieu* is the earliest dated Historic Wreck. However, an empty hull has less to offer in terms of the social history of the period. For the time being archaeological management consists of monitoring visits.

Viewpoint: the River Hamble can be reached by footpath through the woods of the country park
Display: Southampton Maritime Museum has a few timbers and Victorian souvenirs on show
Further reading: Friel, I. et al. 1993. Henry V's *Grace Dieu* and the wreck in the R. Hamble. *International Journal of Nautical Archaeology*, 22.1: 3-51

Mary Rose
Solent, Hampshire

General Location: SZ 6327 9642
Protection: 50° 45' 48"N 01° 06' 10"W, 300m radius
HISTORICAL
Built: 1509 Portsmouth
Type: carrack
Dimensions: 700 tons
Armament: 76 iron; 15 brass
Rebuilt: 1536
Lost: 19 July 1545
Voyage: defending Portsmouth against the French. **Complement:** 185 soldiers; 30 gunners; 200 sailors

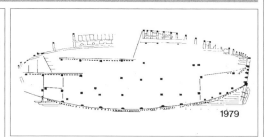

1979

Mary Rose was a successful fighting ship, built in 1509, which served twenty-seven active years before being rebuilt in 1536. Modernisation increased her size and stiffened the hull below the waterline to enable her to carry heavy guns on the main deck. Even as an old ship she was the pride of Henry VIII's fleet. She finally sank in 1545 as she manoeuvred to engage a French fleet in the Solent.

Heeled over in 12m of water half of her hull was entombed in soft anaerobic mud which preserved the whole starboard side and its contents. The hope that the ship survived was based on records of the pioneer divers, John and Charles Deane, who recovered cannon in the nineteenth century. For Alexander McKee finding the *Mary Rose* became a quest. His search was narrowed by discovery of a chart marking the wreck investigated by the Deanes, and by use of the best sonar equipment available in the mid-1960s.

The discovery of the wreck in 1971 was followed by eight seasons of excavation culminating in raising the hull. This was the largest underwater archaeological operation undertaken in Britain. Its success rested on the integration of volunteer divers in a professional programme of excavation. The mammoth logistical task was managed by two deputy directors of archaeology, three full-time dive marshals and four archaeological supervisors, plus log keepers and stand-by divers. More than 500 volunteers took part making over 28,000 dives. In justification of this multi-million pound project, when others were starved of funds, Margaret Rule said, 'it would be vandalism to sink small trenches into the wreck, extract a few objects and then go away without understanding the context within which those objects were used and lost'.

The team recovered more than 19,000 objects of which more than a third are made of wood. This makes *Mary Rose* exceptional, not only in the number and variety of artefacts recovered but in the way groups of objects can be associated with an owner. No fewer than 51 chests, the personal storage of those on board, were preserved. The contents of three of these enabled the cabins in which they were found to be identified respectively as those of the barber surgeon, carpenter and pilot. On the main gundeck bronze and wrought-iron guns on their carriages were in place with their muzzles protruding through the open ports.

Margaret Rule told the story of the *Mary Rose* in a book published in 1982, the year she was brought to the surface and housed in Portsmouth Historic Dockyard. Millions of visitors have already marvelled at the museum displays of tools, domestic objects, games and weapons and looked over the hull. Fifteen years later the full academic publication is still awaited. It will be the culmination of painstaking recording, analysis and conservation.

The site is still designated to protect any material from the collapsed port side and upper works which may survive outside the excavated area. The site is regularly monitored and was recently used to test a new approach to identifying wreck sites even where the main hull structure has been lost. Remote sensing equipment identified now infilled areas of seabed which had once been holes scoured by currents passing the hull.

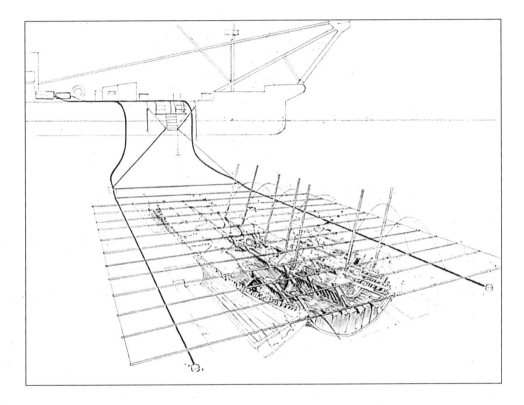

This artist's impression of the seabed by Jonathan Adams shows the surviving half hull, the starboard side, lying in the seabed. The decks become vertical surfaces. Compare this with the 1979 site plan (opposite) where the ends of deck beams were seen as isolated timbers.

Viewpoint: Southsea Castle, where Henry VIII watched his flagship sink
Display: Portsmouth Historic Dockyard houses both the hull and the exhibition of artefacts
Further reading: Rule, M. 1982. *The Mary Rose. The Excavation and Raising of Henry VIII's Flagship.*

The Medieval Ship

For a thousand years ships built of overlapping clinker planks were adequate for England's war and trade. From the king's ship buried at Sutton Hoo about AD 625 to Harold's ships on the Bayeux Tapestry, to vessels shown on medieval town seals, they had in common pointed sterns, quarter rudders, single decks and single masts. The shape of the hull changed with the introduction of the sternpost rudder and transom stern, and larger ships with a higher freeboard and more decks. At first small fighting platforms for archers were constructed fore and aft, but soon these were incorporated into the structure and became towering forecastles and aftercastles. The addition of a foremast and a mizen improved ships' sailing qualities and enabled marksmen to be accommodated high up the mast in fighting tops. The main armament of *Grace Dieu* was the long bow with which Henry V resoundingly won Agincourt three years before her launch. Her guns were small and unreliable, her bows accurate at more than 180m.

Larger designs placed impossible strains on a traditional clinker-built hull. At some point, not documented historically nor yet identified by an archaeological find, the solution was two thicknesses of clinker planking. We only know of this development through the fortunate survival of *Grace Dieu*, the 'ultimate clinker ship'. Another archaeological proof of fifteenth-century technological change was found at Woolwich in 1912. This was almost certainly *Sovereign* which was rebuilt the same year *Mary Rose* was launched. The stump of its mainmast, more than 13ft (4m) in circumference, survived, showing it to be composite, made of oak and pine bound with iron bands. Its frames had notches showing that original clinker planking had been replaced with carvel planking.

Mary Rose was built the new way with a strong skeleton and strong carvel planking. However, her castles were still clinker-planked and she still relied on archers as well as guns for her defence.

Grace Dieu, *modelled by Timothy Concannon. Model-making tests theories. From excavated fragments an idea of the whole ship is built up. Building a scale model can test the practicality of the idea while computers can calculate cargo capacity and sailing performance.*

3 A Ship for All Seasons

'In 1492 Columbus sailed the Ocean Blue.' Atlantic voyages were made possible by the evolution of a more seaworthy vessel with sails on three masts. Following the explorer's lead Europeans voyaged to the New World to exploit its riches, especially silver. The countries tapping into this new wealth could afford to purchase the produce of other European countries. While smaller ships were chosen for exploration larger merchant ships were built to carry home spoils from all parts of the world as well as the increasing European cargoes such as wine, corn, hides, wool and textiles. They could also transport the larger guns needed for their own defence. Their shape and design is known mainly from paintings, but parts of actual hulls have been found on three Historic Wreck sites in south coast anchorages.

Cattewater Wreck
Plymouth Sound, Devon

General Location: SX 4872 5351
Protection: 50° 21' 41.4"N 04° 07' 37.5"W, 50m radius

ARCHAEOLOGICAL

Dimensions: 20m keel (65ft) estimated length
Armament: included cast-iron swivel guns

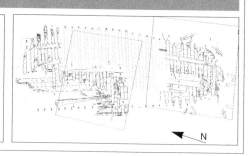

N

In 1973 a dredger, contracted by the Department of the Environment, struck a wooden wreck in the Cattewater, Plymouth. It was just two months after the Protection of Wrecks Act had become law. The discovery triggered a chain of events which met the expectations of those who had fought long and hard for the legislation. Informal cooperation between finders, government departments and national museums made a rapid assessment of the wreck possible.

The Department of the Environment provided a diver, Ken Ellis, to ensure the safe recovery of timbers dragged free by the dredger. He then surveyed what was exposed on the compacted sand seabed at a depth of 9m. The National Maritime Museum sent an archaeological adviser, Valerie Fenwick, and a ship specialist, Eric McKee, to assess the recovered timbers. The guns were taken for conservation and study to the Inspectorate of Ancient Monuments. Following the precedent set by the Museum's handling of the Saxon Graveney boat, within twelve months a report on the Cattewater Wreck was published as a National Maritime Museum monograph. This objective evaluation provided a sound basis for determining the importance of the wreck and planning future research.

Two different teams applied for a licence to continue surveying the site. The Department of Trade tactfully suggested that they might join forces and the Cattewater Wreck Committee was set up. Over the next four seasons, students, volunteers, and divers from Fort Bovisand and the RAF Sub-Aqua Federation partly cleared and carefully mapped some 50% of the remaining hull in poor visibility. A full report of the partial excavation was undertaken as research by Mark Redknap and published in 1984.

Nothing was recovered to precisely identify the wreck, its nationality or its date. Its fast-grown timber was unsuitable for tree-ring dating. However, weighing up all the clues, it seems this was a 200-300 ton armed merchantman built in the early sixteenth century and wrecked about 1530. Of special interest were the three identical early guns. Each gun was made of a wrought-iron tube strengthened with iron rings and secured with iron straps to a tapering oak support, or 'bed'. A separate breech-chamber held the charge, having to be wedged tightly into place between the back of the gun and its bed. A touch hole still had in it the twist of hemp which had kept the powder from getting damp. The whole cumbersome assembly was nearly 2m (6ft) long, with a bore of 55mm (2in), and was designed to swivel on the rail of the ship and be trained by a single gunner using the foresight on its muzzle.

A well-preserved portion of the bottom of the ship showed that its carvel planks of sawn oak had been very carefully fitted needing little caulking. The way the framing of the ship was arranged has much in common with ship finds which date to the period when Europe was building true ocean-going ships to open up the New World. Remains of hearth tiles and cooking debris suggest that the galley was located down in the hold.

The ballast stones piled on top of loose planking (ceiling) over the frames do not have an exotic origin but seem rather to have been picked up at places along the south coast or Severn Estuary.

A range of information about the clothes being worn was found. Fragments of wool fabric had seams and shapes which showed they came from garments. The fine fabrics were too precious for everyday wear with silk threads and pink and purple dyes. Leather shoes, belts, a finely pleated leather purse and what seems to be a cod piece were identified together with a buckle and lace end.

The ship still lies in the Cattewater. 'This goodly rode for great shippes' was at the time of the loss a vital harbour of refuge for the premier naval port in the kingdom.

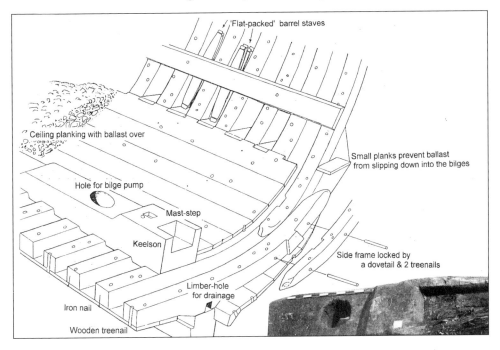

Photograph of the keelson when first recovered and a reconstruction to show its position in the hull. It had a fatter central section to accommodate the mast-step and also a pump well. This would have been a simple bored-out tree-trunk fitted with a leather flap valve, such as was found on the Studland Bay Wreck. Short pieces of plank were inserted between the frames to stop ballast and rubbish from slipping into the bilges, and dismantled barrel staves were neatly packed above them.

Viewpoint: seafront on the newly developed Mount Batten promontory, looking towards the marina

Collections: Plymouth City Museum

Further reading: Redknap. M. 1984. *The Cattewater Wreck. British Archaeological Reports*, 131

Studland Bay (see Colour Plate 4)
Poole, Dorset

General Location: SZ 0614 8468
Protection: 50° 39.67'N 01° 54.79'W, 75m radius

ARCHAEOLOGICAL

Dimensions: estimated length 24m x 5m (80 x 16ft)
Armament: included wrought-iron guns
Cargo: included Spanish pottery

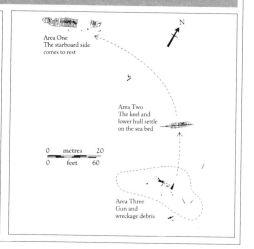

Area One
The starboard side comes to rest

N

Area Two
The keel and lower hull settle on the sea bed

| 0 | metres | 20 |
| 0 | feet | 60 |

Area Three
Gun and wreckage debris

Fishermen using trawls and dredges are well placed to find shipwrecks. Their 'net fastenings' are recorded on charts so that they can be avoided in future. Sometimes nets snag so badly on an underwater obstruction that divers are needed to clear them. This is how Hamworthy SAC divers found the Studland Bay Wreck in 1984. Twelve metres below in exceptionally clear water they could see a carvel-built hull protruding from the sandy bottom. It had been exposed by recent storms. A timber and potsherds were recovered and taken to Poole Museum for identification.

The pottery showed that the shipwreck dated to the early sixteenth century. Shortly afterwards it was designated, and the Hamworthy Club and Poole Maritime Trust set up the Studland Wreck Project (later the Poole Bay Archaeological Research Group) to carry out a scientific pre-disturbance survey. A licence was granted and, with strong local support, nine seasons of work were carried out to a high standard under local archaeological direction. A 28-page colour booklet was published in 1993 and there is a permanent exhibition in Poole Waterfront Museum.

Two main pieces of wreckage were found: the upper starboard side, and the keel with the lower hull and part of the stern assembly. Lying on clay these were covered by deposits no more than 40cm (16in) deep within the overlying sand. It was decided not to raise the timbers. Instead they were carefully excavated and recorded, and then covered with woven polypropylene sheet and sandbagged. A third area had a scatter of wreckage, a gun and small objects. In all 750 artefacts have been recovered and together with the ship structure provide the best example of a Late Medieval merchantman to have been found in the UK.

The structure of the ship has some similarities with the Cattewater Wreck, such as the absence of caulking between its fast-grown oak planking, lap-dovetailed lower frames, and similar combination of wood and metal fastenings. It had a rounded stem, a transom stern and rather flat sides above and below its bilge. A walnut pump base with a leather valve was found sitting on the keel and iron bolts showed where the keelson would have fitted. Guns of two sizes were found: a large breech-loader made of iron staves and fastened to its carriage by iron bands; and a 100mm (4in) swivel gun. This has a much larger bore than

Mike Markey with the largest gun from the wreck, a 'port piece' 2m (6ft) long loaded with a stone shot. With a bore of 180mm (7in) it would have pierced an enemy ship. The Spanish pottery provides rare dating for this early iron gun. The only similar guns known in Britain are one in Tenby Museum and those found aboard Mary Rose.

the Cattewater guns and a significantly more advanced design, since it does not require a wooden support to secure its chamber.

Unlike the Cattewater Wreck this ship was ballasted with foreign stone. About 50% of it was from the Basque region of northern Spain. What clinched the Spanish connection were the colourful ceramics on board. These were of different types and appeared to have been part of a pottery cargo along with perishables in barrels. About 20 pieces of golden lustreware made in Valencia, and known to have been admired and coveted in Europe, may have been on its way to be traded in south coast ports together with wine in the barrels. More exotic still and not normally traded in Europe were a similar number of purple and blue tin-glazed plates. They were made near Seville and date to c.1500-25. This type of plate was taken to the West Indies by early colonists and has been found in Isabela, a settlement founded in Dominica by Columbus.

Other items would have been used by those on board: lice combs, an ointment pot, shoes and rush matting. There was chopped firewood and simple pottery for cooking, while beef, mutton and pork bones together with wheat, pepper and fig seeds tell of their meals.

Full publication of the Studland Bay wreck would give this site the recognition it deserves. A very large part of a probably Spanish ship is preserved. It dates from the time when Iberian ships were opening up the world's oceans, but when very little is known of the achievements in ship construction which made this possible.

Viewpoint: the naturist beach at Studland can be reached via the path through the dunes of the Nature Reserve. The site is buoyed
Display: Waterfront Museum, Poole
Further reading: Ladle, L. undated. *The Studland Bay Wreck*. Poole Museum Heritage Series No.1

Yarmouth Roads
Yarmouth, Isle of Wight

General Location: SZ 3577 9007
Protection: 50° 42.520'N 01° 29.597'W, 50m
radius
ARCHAEOLOGICAL
Dimensions: suggested length 32m (105ft)

Discovery of the Yarmouth Roads Wreck was certainly a surprise. It lies in sight of the castle which Henry VIII built to defend the town from invaders. Yet, despite the wreck being less than 200m from the shore and in only 6m of water, local records do not mention a ship being lost near the town.

The site is among the few Historic Wrecks discovered during an archaeological survey of the seabed. It was found in 1984 by volunteer divers who were looking for the source of some Roman pottery trawled up by local oyster fishermen. The survey had been requested by the Isle of Wight Archaeological Unit which was already involved with the *Pomone/Assurance* Historic Wreck site. Everything combined to convince the County Archaeologist, David Tomalin, that the Island's history lay as much in the sea as on the land. The search of historical records for a ship to match the Yarmouth Wreck was developed by Alison Gale into a pioneering inventory of wreck sites and artefacts from the seabed around the Isle of Wight.

The resulting Maritime Sites & Monuments Record contained hundreds of accounts of ship losses, reports of objects brought up by fishermen and shipwrecks actually located on the seabed. Similar records have since been created by coastal counties and, following a government instruction in 1992, nationally for England, Scotland, Northern Ireland and Wales. These inventories are the only gauge of the total ships lost, and wrecks found, against which to judge the merit of the forty seven Historic Wrecks.

Fittingly it was records of central government written four centuries earlier which provided the long-awaited identity of the Yarmouth Roads Wreck. In 1567 the High Court of Admiralty had heard the petition of a Spanish merchant, Antonio de Gwarras, seeking from the Captain of the Isle of Wight, Sir Edward Horsey, the return of wool salvaged from the *Santa Lucia*. She was bound for Flanders when she perished 'thwart of Yarmouthe'. Through the centuries there were so few wrecks in the area that this match seems convincing. Unfortunately, seabed excavations have not found anything to prove the case, but there is evidence in favour of *Santa Lucia*.

The shallow ledge on which the Yarmouth Roads Wreck lies is eroding. It does not have the deep sediments of the eastern Solent which preserved so much of *Mary Rose* and *Invincible*. Only in hollows no deeper than 1.5m (5ft) were large fragments of hull found lying under protective sediments. The keel and bottom of the ship had already disappeared, but collapsed parts of the stern and sides appeared to have literally dug their own graves by rocking abrasively on the hard clay. The few recovered artefacts are mainly ceramic, lead or pewter, copper alloy and wood. No leather or textiles have been found. Three stone shot were the only hint of armament, although a superb bronze gun with its wooden carriage was found about 150m to the east. This was cast in Venice by Zuane Alberghetti some time after 1582.

In the identification of a shipwreck key clues are initials and crests with which pewter and silver tableware was often marked. These have removed all doubt about the identity of documented ships like *Coronation*, *Royal Anne* and *Stirling Castle*. However, none of the marks on the Yarmouth Roads pewter vessels could be identified and, even worse, the scarcity of early pewter made it difficult to date the first few plates from their shape. Gradually as more pewter vessels were recovered together with Genoese tin-glazed pottery it became possible to place the shipwreck in the middle of the 16th century.

Since the wreck was not under threat only limited excavation was undertaken. This was achieved by a team funded through the Manpower Services Commission supported by volunteer divers. This source of funding ended in 1989. Since then the site has been monitored.

Viewpoint: Yarmouth Pier or Yarmouth Common (top left). Yarmouth Roads is a traditional anchorage and modern yachts lie off the old town. The Historic Wreck buoy is a yellow sphere (bottom), made white by sea gull droppings.

Display: Fort Victoria; Collections: Isle of Wight Archaeological Unit
Further Reading: Watson, K. & Gale, A. 1990. Site Evaluation for marine sites and monuments records: The Yarmouth Roads Wreck investigations. *International Journal of Nautical Archaeology*, 19.3: 183-192; Williams, D. 1991. *Salvage. Rescued from the Deep.*

Ballast

Wind and waves cause a ship to roll and pitch. To improve stability ballast placed in the bottom of a vessel lowered the centre of gravity. Frequently it took the place of discharged cargo. When possible a cheap saleable commodity, such as bricks, was taken on board a merchantman to ballast a lightweight cargo, such as silks or tobacco.

The foul air rising from stinking bilges is hard to imagine today, but was often described. It pervaded the whole ship and constituted a major health hazard. Officers and important passengers were accommodated in airy cabins in the stern - upwind in a sailing ship. The lieutenant on *Dartmouth* complained that the ballast and bilges was 'stinking and all of a quagmire', clogging the waterways. He commented that if the ballast was taken out and clean shingle put in 'doubt not but our ship would be healthy and in a good condition'. This operation, known as 'rummaging' involved heaving a ship down in some convenient spot and offloading her ballast so that the hold could be scrubbed and the ballast washed by the tide.

A low mound of stones on the seabed is often the only visible evidence of a wreck site. Like other archaeological material, ballast can tell us much and, unlike commodities of value, it was seldom salvaged. Thus its total weight and disposition indicates the size or class of vessel. The ballast components may have a precise geological origin and this can point to where it was taken on board, as in the case of the Cattewater and Studland Bay ballast.

The type of material used as ballast can help to provide a rough period for an unidentified vessel. Sand and small stones used as ballast provided a large surface area for the growth of algae, bacteria, and fungi, which combined to make the stench. In addition it was laborious to handle and clogged pumps and drainage channels. For this reason, after about 1600, larger-size stone ballast was used in the English navy. Lead ingots, stone shot, old guns and broken anchors were also used. In the eightenth century the increasing weight of iron guns carried by warships above the waterline was offset by iron ballast cast both to fixed dimensions and with lifting holes.

4 Discoveries, Dates & Doubts

The majority of shipwrecks have been found by divers making 'eyeball' contact on the seabed. Guns of iron or bronze are heavy and robust and these enduring objects often give divers the first clue to a wreck site. Metal ingots cast in regular shapes for easy transport are another common find. While some guns and ingots carry inscriptions or stamps which give accurate dates, many are unmarked. Increasingly, researchers of particular objects, be it guns, ingots or even clay pipes, rely on well-documented shipwrecks to fit accurate dates to chronologies which they have built up using largely the physical characteristics of their chosen artefacts. For some sites where little more than guns or ingots have so far been recovered or reported it is not yet possible to suggest a precise date for the ship's loss.

St. Anthony (see Colour Plate 3)
Gunwalloe, Cornwall

General Location: SW 6490 2264
Protection: 50° 03.4'N 05° 17.1'W, 75m radius
HISTORICAL
Type: 'fine ship'
Armament: bronze and iron cannon
Lost: 19 January 1527
Voyage: Flanders to Lisbon
Cargo: silver, copper, metal goods
Saved: crew and passengers except 41, cargo subject to Court of Star Chamber proceedings

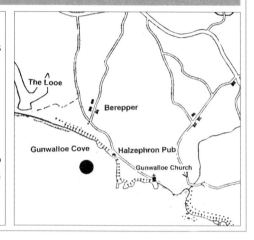

The wreck of *St Anthony* at Gunwalloe in 1527 is extremely well-documented. Yet her discovery in 1981 was unexpected by local wreck divers. The road from the Halzephron pub leads to a beach and it was here that a local man found a copper ingot. His work colleague, Anthony Randall, was a diver and guessed that it had been washed up from a wreck. For the find was made at the end of Looe Bar, which from the sea appears to be a long beach where ships in distress could run ashore. However, the sea shallows some 230m offshore and great rock reefs have torn many ships apart.

St Anthony carried bullion and her discovery featured in *Diver Magazine*. Swimming off the beach Anthony Randall found more copper ingots. When a metal detector search revealed dozens more, thoughts turned to *St Anthony*. Divers believed she would be found in the rocky coves to the south-west, closer to the present Gunwalloe Church. The identity was clinched by a solid silver ingot, shaped as a half melon and weighing 8kg ($17\frac{1}{2}$ lb). *St Anthony*'s cargo list included 18 such 'cakes' of silver.

St Anthony was bound from Flanders as the flagship of a fleet. Her loss was followed by violent disagreements between the survivors and local people over salvage. A Cornish historian summed up the problem in the local attitude: 'wrecks were regarded as manifestations of God's grace and as a hereditary right'. As *St Anthony* belonged to, or was chartered by, England's ally, King John III of Portugal, it was in the interests of Henry VIII's diplomacy to see the dispute settled. Her cargo is recorded in a petition made to Henry. It was principally metals: 8000 cakes of copper; 3200 latten candlesticks; 2100 barbers' basins; 3 sets of silver tableware; precious stones and jewels, brass and iron guns. There were also rich cloths and a chest of musical instruments. The ship and cargo were valued at £18,880.

Under John III, Portugal became enormously prosperous by opening the direct sea route to the East and trading pepper through Antwerp, thus destroying Venice's monopoly based on the overland spice route. Portuguese merchants required silver and metalwork to exchange for eastern goods. These they acquired in Antwerp, the great mart and banking centre of Europe.

The wreck was designated in 1982 and licences for survey and excavation have been issued throughout the '80s and '90s. Survey began in 1983 but a magnetometer failed to locate the one cannon seen previously on the site. Work in the rocky outcrops and gullies was cut short by the gales and the heavy Atlantic swell which hit the site and destroy visibility. The area is also prone to sand movement which can conceal wrecks for long periods. A display in Charlestown Shipwreck & Heritage Centre is representative of the artefacts, recovery of which has been reported in *Diver Magazine* and the *Nautical Archaeology Society Newsletter*. These are the silver ingots and copper ingots, candlesticks, stink pots, sounding lead, and pieces of cast brass.

Academic interest has only focused on the ingots, the British Museum having acquired examples of both silver and copper from the wreck. Analysis of the copper produced unexpected information. The *St Anthony* copper, smelted about 1527, had as little as 0.06% nickel. This raises doubts about the assumption, used for dating, that a nickel content under 0.1% indicated a pre-1300 date for copper alloy objects.

The church in the dunes at Gunwalloe Cove has six painted wooden panels of saints. Analysis of the paint, the style of painting and the subjects all point to these being sixteenth-century Iberian painted panels salvaged from *St Anthony*.

Viewpoint: the wreck site is clearly marked by a metal notice on the small wall at the beach entrance. It can also be viewed as part of Looe Bar from Halzephron Headland.

Display: Charlestown Shipwreck & Heritage Centre
Further reading: Chynoweth,I. 1968. The wreck of the St Anthony. *Journal of the Royal Institute of Cornwall*, 5.4: 385-406 (historical); Larn, R & B. 1995. *Shipwreck Index of the British Isles*. Volume 1 (listing)

Rill Cove
The Lizard, Cornwall

General Location: SW 6767 1345

Protection: 49° 58′ 31.0″N 05° 14′ 26.7″W, 100m radius
ARCHAEOLOGICAL

Armament: included iron swivel guns

Lost: after 1603/5

Cargo: included silver coins

The Historic Wreck in Rill Cove is unidentified. It has remained nameless despite being linked with a vessel whose loss has been recorded in the historic papers of the Duchy of Cornwall. Unfortunately, the lack of information in modern archaeological and diving publications leaves the wreck site itself to be almost as mysterious as the lost ship.

On 8 March 1618 a letter from the Duchy of Cornwall mentioned 'certain bars of silver taken up out of the sea at the Lizard'. During the next ten years the papers of the Duchy include reports of more silver being recovered from the Lizard. The only hint at a more precise position comes when Sir John Killigrew is building a lighthouse and the salvage is said to be from a ship wrecked nearby. A hint of the ship's value and origin comes in 1628. The famous salvor and pioneer diver, Jacob Johnson, sought permission to work on a ship wrecked about nine years earlier at the Lizard and laden with silver bars and pieces of eight from 'St Lucar'.

Just as place-names had deceived those seeking the *St Anthony* so those hopeful of finding the documented silver wreck were misled into believing that she would be found on the Lizard Headland itself. Her discovery was, as is so often the case, a complete chance.

It was 1975 when Ken Simpson and Mike Hall were diving on the *Kerris Reed*, a trawler wrecked against the cliffs in the 1960s. In about 9m of water in Rill Cove they spotted iron guns. The site was designated because the guns were believed to date to the late 1500s and Spanish coins from the site were dated to the sixteenth and seventeenth centuries.

Ken Simpson described the difficulties of investigating the wreck. By April 1976 strong ground seas had deposited sand to a depth of 3.6m (12ft). While the sand was only 1.2-1.5m (4-5ft) deep a hand-held magnetometer had been used to find the limits of the site. This showed it was relatively small in area but that artefacts were scattered over the whole of it. The western extremity could not be established because the metal remains of the *Kerris Reed* lay over it. It was prohibitively costly to attempt to dig through the deep sand to complete survey work. While licences have been issued little has been undertaken in recent seasons.

The *Kerris Reed* overlying the wreck site is typical of the seabed around the Lizard Peninsula where divers readily speak of metal hulls above timbers and cast-iron guns. The four Historic Wrecks around its rocks and coves must under-represent the number of

Viewpoint: a visit to Kynance Cove, reached via the National Trust toll road, may suggest why this treasure ship was lost without a name. From the beach, at low tide on a calm day, you can look out past the massive, craggy stack called the Bellows to Rill Cove. Alternatively, take the cliff path to look down into the remote cove. In a winter storm its rocky cliffs lashed by wind and crashing Atlantic waves would offer no safety to seamen struggling from a breaking ship.

ships which it has taken as casualties. Like the Goodwins, the Needles and the Isles of Scilly it is a long-standing accident blackspot for shipping.

One built-up banded iron cannon was recovered, measured and salvaged and then replaced underwater. Some small artefacts have also been recovered including pewter buttons, sounding leads, lead bottle seals and unidentified copper alloy objects. Porthleven Wreck & Rescue has a small display which shows the location of the site and a sample of the recovered coins. These are silver pieces of eight, four, two and one, unmilled coins from the mints of Potosi in Mexico, Seville and Toledo. They fall into two datable groups, of 1555-98 and 1598-1603/5. It is a large group with over 400 recovered coins. Study of dated wrecks shows that treasure ships, like the Spanish *Atocha* wrecked on the Florida Keys in 1622, have coins from their year of loss and, with smaller coin groups, the gap between the last minted coin and the loss of the ship is commonly under six years.

Display: Porthleven Wreck & Rescue
Further reading: Simpson, K. et al. 1977. An early seventeenth century wreck near Rill Cove, Kynance, Cornwall. An interim report. *International Journal of Nautical Archaeology*, 2.6: 163-6

Bartholomew Ledge (see Colour Plate 3), Isles of Scilly, Cornwall

General Location: SV 8911 0953
Protection: 49° 54.26'N 06° 19.83'W, 100m radius

ARCHAEOLOGICAL

Lost: after 1555
Armament: included iron guns
Cargo: included bell metal and lead ingots as cargo or ballast

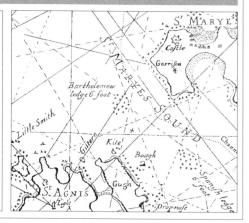

Finding the ship's bell is every diver's dream and the answer, or at least a clue, to a ship's name. Finding 644 fragments of bell was something no-one had imagined possible. Their origin is still a subject of conjecture.

Mike Pirie ran diving holidays from St Mary's. Wrecks were his business and there was no undue excitement when, in 1979, he found some lead ingots on Bartholomew Ledge. The Ledge lies dangerously close to the surface in St Mary's Sound and has seen at least seven recorded wreckings. However, as he began finding fragments of bronze bell, anchors and guns he sought advice from Roy Graham. An application for protection was made in September 1980 and the site was designated on 3 October.

When, two days later, poor weather ended the diving season information on the site could be summarised as: recovered bell fragments weighing more than a ton (1224kg); 4 iron breech-loading guns and some iron anchors left on site; 13 pottery sherds sent for identification; a number of lead ingots stored on a small island; 2 small lead shot and an unidentified lead object; and a piece of concretion carrying the impression of a seal.

A local archaeologist and craftsman, Humphrey Wakefield, reported his observations of the bell fragments. They were all a 'handy' size, the largest weighing only 30lb (15.9kg). Many were covered in a fine clay some of which was overlain by a black material, which he considered was probably plumbago, a release agent used in traditional bell casting. It showed the detail of the original mould, but the poor delineation of the lettering suggested that the bronze had not always 'filled' the mould properly. He concluded that the fragments were deliberately broken pieces of faulty castings, rejects from the foundry floor transported as cargo or ballast.

The idea that the Ledge was named after an Armada ship, the *San Bartolome* has been questioned. Only two Armada ships carrying the saint's name have been traced, one from 1588 and one from 1597, neither is recorded lost on the Isles of Scilly. Further research suggests Bishop Bartholomew as the origin, hence the absence of the 'Saint' prefix.

A survey licence was granted in 1981. After clearance of weed, the only further sign of the wreck was one more lead ingot. The team suggested that a 1906 wreck, *Magdalene*, might obscure the early wreck as at Rill Cove, or that remains were buried by rocks and shingle. A magnetometer was used without success to search for any dispersed wreckage to the south and east of the main site. The 1982 survey followed similar lines and with equally unpromising results. While the team felt no progress would be made without excavation, a suitable licence was only issued in 1986.

No investigation has been licensed since then and, as with *St Anthony*, the ingots are the only objects to have attracted academic attention. The British Museum has acquired one ingot but has so far not traced the origin of its ore. Of the 105 ingots reportedly recovered very few have found their way to local museums. Only 10 bell fragments have been traced. Most of the lead and bronze was disposed of for its metal and the wreck itself remains a mystery. Six coins, originally passed to Charlestown Shipwreck & Heritage Centre provide some dating: 4 two-reales of Ferdinand & Isabella (1474-1504); a half reale of Emperor Charles (1521-55), and a thaler of 1555. These were not the 'pieces of eight' used as bullion, but coins for currency and may be close in date to the time of the shipwreck.

Spoils of War

'Those places which doe stand out after summons given, doe forfeit their Bells to the Generall of the Ordinance...by the Custome of Warr.' Bells were an invaluable source of metal for armaments and from the Medieval Period until World War II they were carried away by conquering forces as 'Military Perquisites'. An explanation for the presence of so much broken bell metal, together with between 4.5 and 6 tonnes of lead, is that this represents deliberately smashed bells and lead melted down after capture in war and en route to a gun foundry. The Lombardic lettering on surviving fragments suggests that some of these bells were cast before c.1420. The lead ingots from the site varied between 45 and 60 kg (100-130lb) in weight and were apparently unmarked. Their shape is known to metallurgists as 'wedge'.

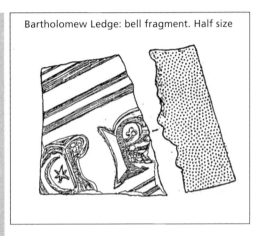

Bartholomew Ledge: bell fragment. Half size

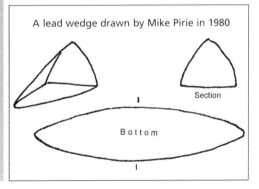

A lead wedge drawn by Mike Pirie in 1980

Section

Bottom

Viewpoint: The Garrison, St Mary's, the redoubt on the south side gives a low-level view of St Mary's Sound
Display: Longstone Heritage Centre (2 ingots only); Charlestown Shipwreck & Heritage Centre (ingots only)
Collections: St Mary's Museum (bell fragments)

Gull Rock
Lundy, Devon

General Location: SS 1435 4630

Protection: 51° 11.11'N 04° 39.41'W, 100m radius

ARCHAEOLOGICAL

Armament: included wrought-iron guns

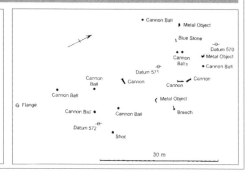

Excellent visibility and exceptional seabed flora and fauna attract divers to Lundy. The Island also has around 20 wreck dives but two sites are out of bounds to divers, Gull Rock and *Iona II*.

The Gull Rock Wreck was relocated in 1983, fifteen years after it was originally reported by John Shaw. It lies on the sheltered east side of the Island at the base of a rocky slope in some 25m of water. A recent survey mapped the visible objects: 2 wrought-iron cannon, a breech-loading gun and 8 limestone cannon balls. More modern items were assumed to have come from nearby wrecks.

The seabed is soft silt and the possibility that it preserves more of the wreck was one reason for the site being designated in 1990. However, no excavation has been permitted to test this theory. In 1994, for example, a request was refused to lift a gun to assist in identifying and dating the ship. This was understandable as iron objects are difficult to conserve, and the favoured option on sites such as Tearing Ledge and *Dartmouth* was to record iron guns on the seabed. For Gull Rock there is the additional consideration that disturbing the seabed is against the ethos of the Marine Nature Reserve in which it lies.

Wrecks and Coastal Management

The coast is a complex market, a place of supply and demand. For most people the coast is known only as a place for holidays, sport and relaxation. It is difficult for the coast to supply the 'unspoilt', 'clean' character which they demand while also supporting the operations which supply other coastal resources in heavy demand – fish, sand and gravel, dumps for waste, oil and gas, room for marinas, and space for housing and industry. The interests of all these different activities are represented by different industries and are regulated by many different government departments and non-government agencies.

One solution to the conflicting demands is called Coastal Zone Management, CZM for short. The idea is to look at the whole coast and to seek the best possible options for meeting everyone's needs both now and in the future. This may mean some activities have to be curtailed or restricted to certain areas.

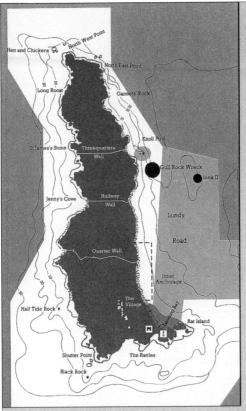

In Britain there is increasing interest and activity in coordinated management of the coast but, so far, CZM has not been implemented by law as one holistic solution. In the past laws have been enacted which allow defined areas of seabed to be managed for specific reasons. The Protection of Wrecks Act (1973) is an example of this type of law. Another is the Wildlife & Countryside Act (1981) which made it possible to create Marine Nature Reserves. These cover much larger areas and show how 'zoning' can be used to integrate different sea and seabed activities.

The Lundy Marine Nature Reserve is the responsibility of English Nature. It has a warden, and an interpretation centre. Information is expected to help the public to enjoy and treat with respect the marine flora and fauna. A leaflet explains that the zoning scheme works 'for the benefit of both wildlife and people, by showing users where they can undertake activities with minimal impact on natural features and on each other'.

Shipwrecks within the Reserve are valued as wildlife habitats. Visiting divers are encouraged to leave them untouched and record their observations in the Lundy Log Book. In contrast the two designated Historic Wrecks are out of bounds, the only areas in the Reserve where diving is prohibited. On a personal level wardens have felt that the Historic Wrecks leave two holes in their responsibility, but on an organisational level English Nature has no remit or resources for managing archaeological sites. The possibility of the warden becoming licensee and so taking responsibility for visits to the wrecks has been discussed, but a workable arrangement has yet to be found.

In 1994 a report was prepared on the seabed archaeology of the Reserve. It highlighted the opportunities for proactive management of all the wrecks in the Reserve: survey and monitoring to record their condition and safeguard vulnerable artefacts; safety measures such as removing fishing gear which might entangle divers; and leaflets, dive trails and seabed signs to encourage responsible visits by divers. Unfortunately resources are not available to implement such schemes.

Viewpoint: the site lies offshore but can be viewed from the coastal path
Further reading: Robertson, P. 1994. Marine Archaeology & Lundy Marine Nature Reserve - an assessment. *Lundy Field Society,* 45: 57-76

Erme Estuary
Bigbury Bay, Devon

General Location: SX 6093 4710

Protection: 50° 18.41′N 03° 57.19′W, 250m radius

The wind is merciless to sailing ships blinded by fog or rain, leaking, with damaged sails, lost rudders, or exhausted crews struggling against exceptional gales. Like helpless autumn leaves they scud along until their passage is barred by some obstacle; the wind passes on but the leaves drop in an untidy pile. The Erme Estuary in Bigbury Bay is one of those places on the British coast where the wind deposited ships in equally jumbled wreck sites.

The West Country coast sweeps in a great arc: after passing the Lizard ships must keep south to clear Start Point, otherwise they will be driven into Bigbury Bay to be wrecked. Ships in Bigbury Bay, like HMS *Pygmy* in 1793, have run for the Erme, mistaking Burgh Island for the Great Mewstone at the entrance to the safe haven of Plymouth Sound. It is a very different place. A reef is strung across the estuary barring passage, save through the western channel, to the 7m of safe water beyond. A strange ship seeking shelter in rough weather would know nothing of the reef until it ripped its bottom out. At least ten ships are known to have met this fate.

From the cliffs above the estuary mouth, at low tide in clear weather, you can see the sand bar across the river and beyond white water breaking over two patches of the reef, East and West St Mary's Rocks. The Historic Wreck lies just north-west of the former. It should be no surprise that the remains cannot be attributed to a single ship.

Divers often explored the reef and flat sand around, and there was talk of guns found and raised. However in 1990, Stephen George found a cluster of iron guns 400m north of the rocks. He sought the help of Neville Oldham and Dave Illingworth. There were four cannon about 2.4m (8ft) long and one smaller gun. They raised the small wrought-iron swivel gun. During conservation, helped by radiography, it was found to be complete with black flint shot in the remains of a bag, and even a decorative spliced rope on the tiller. At that time it was dated to 1450-1550. Eager to investigate the area the group formed the Bigbury Bay Investigation Team, now the South-West Maritime Archaeological Group. An application for protection was turned down by the Department of Transport pending more information from the site.

Work resumed in February 1991 and baselines were laid for survey. The sand level had dropped and revealed a second swivel gun which was raised. One of the large cast-iron guns was also raised. This was a Swedish finbanker dating to 1690-1720 and reaffirmed the idea that there was more than one shipwreck. Responsibility for Historic Wrecks had, by now, passed to the Department of the Environment. A second application for protection was successful and the remaining season was devoted to a predisturbance survey under licence.

Excavation of trial areas did not find any ship structure. The finds have come from the mobile sand which overlies compacted sand and rock. They are difficult to date precisely and include: an unusual deadeye; bar shot; a bronze pestle which would have been used for grinding gunpowder; a bronze pan weight which was stamped in the reign of Charles I; and a badly worn figurine. Currently the build-up of sand precludes further investigation.

In 1994 the team won the Duke of Edinburgh's Prize for the British Sub Aqua Club for their work on the adjacent tin ingot site, also within the estuary mouth. The award is made in recognition of an outstanding achievement and research in the field of underwater swimming. In addition to the Erme Estuary sites the team is also responsible for the discovery and investigation of the Salcombe Cannon Wreck.

Viewpoint: the South West Coast Path provides a good vantage point on the east side of the estuary.

Display: The South-West Maritime Archaeological Group loan artefacts for display in the museum in Salcombe

Further reading: Oldham, N. et al. 1993. The Erme Estuary, Devon, Historic Wreck Site, 1991-3. *International Journal of Nautical Archaeology*, 22.4: 323-30

Brighton Marina
Brighton, East Sussex

General Location: TQ 3328 0294
Protection: 50° 48′ 36.5″N 00° 06′ 29.0″W,
200m E-W x 150m N-S
           ARCHAEOLOGICAL
Armament: included bronze and wrought-iron guns

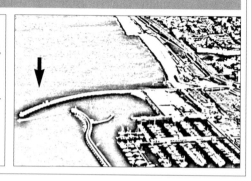

Thirty-five years ago a fifteenth/sixteenth-century bronze gun was acquired by the Tower of London. David Berry had found the minion, reportedly with two more, off Black Rock on the east side of Brighton. By the time that Basildon SAC dived the area in 1974 the scenery was very different. The massive western breakwater of Brighton Marina was nearing completion. The first 3000-ton caisson was positioned in 1972 and the final construction would stretch 630m into the sea.

The Black Cats, as the Basildon divers are known, discovered further guns about 100m from the Marina wall. Several were recovered in 1977. These included a wrought-iron, stave-built gun without its breech chamber. It is not clear whether the nine pieces of rope wrapped around the barrel were part of deck-lashings or tackles or if they were left by some contemporary salvage attempt. A breech chamber was recovered separately along with shot and the remains of three swivels. Perhaps the most telling discovery was a hakbut. While it is difficult to narrow the date for the iron ordnance this bronze gun was dated to c.1475.

In 1982 a further stave-built gun was lifted. This was still mounted on the remains of a wooden 'carriage' and there was a twist of hemp in its touch hole, a wooden tampion in the breech chamber and a stone cannon ball in the barrel.

Despite an earlier application by the team, the site was not designated until 1983. The following season was devoted to surveying 3000 square metres of the chalk bottom with its sand-filled gullies. In depths of 6m metal detectors were used to scan portions of seabed gridded in 3m squares. Licence was only for survey but 'preliminary excavations were undertaken on buried contacts to establish where possible the nature of the find'. This soon posed a problem. Two heavily concreted breech chambers were discovered which the team had no permission to lift. Fearing that they would now be vulnerable to both storms and rogue divers they had to obtain special authority from the Department of Transport to lift them.

Since the ordnance was found in a general west – east line it has been suggested that the main wreck lay in the area now covered by the Marina. This speculation has been fuelled by reports that dredgers and divers clearing the seabed in advance of the western arm removed 'timbers and fastenings'. Wrecks are not the only seabed structures and the remains of the Volks Railway can be seen at low tide. This nineteenth-century engineering innovation carried tourists in carriages on stilts, safely above the sea. It crossed the Marina site and would have had to be removed by the clearance operations.

Ernest Perry's log for his dive on 16 June 1984 at Brighton Marina. Many of the Historic Wrecks have been discovered and investigated entirely by sport divers working in their spare time. Their logs are the primary record of their seabed observation, the methods which they used in the investigation and the problems which they encountered. Their commitment is remarkable. Working at weekends and in holidays, always dependent on weather, it can take years to complete a basic survey. Seabed hours can run into hundreds and even thousands. Seabed archaeology is an expensive hobby. There are personal equipment, boats and archaeological aids to acquire; transport for every site visit; paper and computer records to make and store; and once excavation commences objects to have conserved, identified, dated and finally housed.

Increasingly high-tech solutions are being used to complete initial surveys. Remote sensing equipment can pick out anomalies on the seabed which can then be targeted by divers for closer inspection. This enables more to be achieved for each man-hour on the seabed. The teams investigating Historic Wreck sites have no automatic access to archaeological funding and usually have to find survey companies willing to carry out remote sensing as sponsorship.

Funding could allow newly discovered sites to be immediately surveyed using the most advanced equipment supported by experienced archaeological divers. This would provide the Advisory Committee on Historic Wreck Sites with more complete information to help decide if a site should be designated and would save local teams many hours by providing a sound basis from which to continue survey.

Viewpoint: from Brighton the modern Volks railway, seawall walkway or higher promenade lead to the marina where the site can be seen just to the west

Display: Shipwreck Heritage Centres in Hastings and Charlestown have guns and breeches

Seabed Development & Archaeology

Brighton Marina is an engineering solution to a 500-year-old problem: a port without a harbour. It demonstrates the modern ability to develop the seabed and its resources. To build a marina Brighton Borough Council obtained an Act of Parliament and purchased the freehold of the seabed. Before construction started there was just open sea with rolling waves crashing onto the narrow beach beneath the chalk cliffs. Two breakwaters, 630m and 1220m long, were built to enclose 126 acres (51 ha). Then the marina-village was claimed from the sea, providing 35 acres (14ha) of land for shops and houses. The preparatory dredging, the breakwater construction and land fill may well have destroyed fragile wreck or other archaeological remains. There was no requirement to monitor the construction.

The seabed like the land is strictly controlled. It is mainly managed by the Crown Estate Commissioners. They can lease or sell areas of seabed. They can also authorise activities such as prospecting for, and extracting, sand and gravel, oil and gas. Other organisations control activities such as shipping, fishing or sewage outfalls. Thus at sea there is still no single planning system as is used on land to regulate all development from an individual house to a multi-acre airport.

The planning system on land helps to protect archaeological remains. Guidance issued by the government advocates the preservation of archaeological sites. Developers are expected to undertake desk-top and field studies ahead of development to locate archaeological remains and determine the best means of accommodating them. If it is impractical to preserve them *in situ* then recording is expected.

The archaeology of the seabed does not have the same safeguards. Engineering companies and organisations, such as port authorities, are increasingly aware of the importance of seabed archaeology and have voluntarily begun to include it in their project preparations. However, there is much more to be done to ensure that the physical remains of the maritime past are not unwittingly destroyed.

5 Armada Puzzles

In 1588 the King of Spain brought together warships and merchant ships, old and new, purpose-built and hired, into an Armada to send against England. Victims of violent weather, less than half of the 130-strong fleet returned. From wreck sites in Scotland and Ireland a wealth of personal possessions, ordnance and ships' fittings have been recovered by divers. Only one identified Armada wreck has been designated in United Kingdom waters. In the 1980s a further wreck on the Armada route was found and similarly protected. Its guns and objects are remarkably similar to those from the Irish shipwrecks. In 1994 a second site with comparable guns was found off the Suffolk coast. However, neither of these wreck sites accord with documented losses in the 1588 campaign.

Girona (see Colour Plate 5)
Lacada Point, Antrim

General Location: Irish Grid C 9528 4555
Protection: 55° 14.85'N 06° 30.05'W, 300m radius

HISTORICAL

Built: Naples
Type: galleass
Dimensions: approximately 200ft (61m)
Armament: 50 guns
Lost: 27 October 1588
Voyage: Spain to England, and return to Spain
Complement: Nearly 1300 people comprising her own crew plus survivors of two earlier shipwrecks
Saved: 5 people

As the 7 mile (11km) wide crescent of the Spanish invasion force sailed up the Channel in August 1588 what the English most feared were the four mighty galleasses, red-painted 600-tonners which guarded its extremities.

The galleass was the latest solution to the age-old problem in war at sea–dependence on wind power. It was a combination sailing ship and oared galley, built on a larger scale than ever before in order to pack a punch with its 50 guns. In battle 300 men, including slaves and convicts, could man its oars in shifts so as to avoid the broadsides of the English galleons and bring its heavy forward-facing guns to bear on their vulnerable sterns.

While this strategy might be successful in Mediterranean waters, it did not take account of the stormy seas which the Armada encountered from the time it set sail. For a start the lateen rig had to be changed to squaresails, and rudder-fixings were a continual problem. The capitana (flagship) galleass, *San Lorenzo,* broke her rudder and ran aground at Calais, but two of the others eventually returned to Spain.

The loss of the third, *Girona,* was the greatest single disaster in the campaign. Nearly 1300 Spaniards drowned. In freezing fog at dawn, five months after setting out from Lisbon, she had lost her rudder for the third time and was swept by a gale onto the rocks off the Giant's Causeway. Only five people made it ashore.

Girona had been overloaded, crammed with the gear and survivors of two other Armada ships wrecked nearby. The drinking water was foul and biscuit was rationed to a mere $\frac{1}{2}$lb per day. What had been planned as an advance up the Channel, to land an invasion force on the south coast, had turned into a nightmare flight northwards. In an effort to round Scotland and return to Spain via the North Atlantic numerous ships were wrecked by continuing gales.

The galleasses are the best-documented vessels in the Armada, and after years of research a Belgian diver, Robert Stenuit, became convinced that *Girona* had been lost somewhere on Lacada Point. The ancient place-name 'Port na Spaniagh' was an important clue. On 27 June 1967 he was diving off the jagged rocks in a forest of swaying seaweed

Plate 1

Above: a variety of Bronze Age axes, adzes, chisels and gouges were copied and fitted with hafts to create the full-size section of the Dover Boat.
Below: an adze being used to trim one of the laths secured by yew stitches.

Plate 2

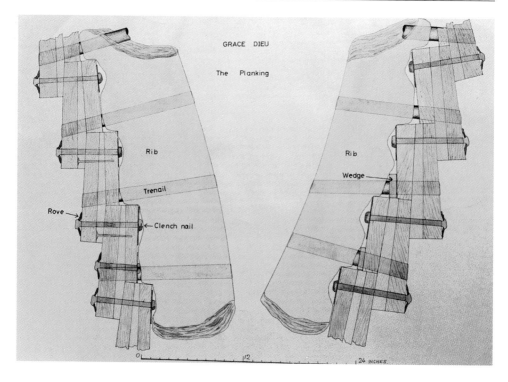

GRACE DIEU

The Planking

Rib

Rib

Wedge

Trenail

Rove

Clench nail

0   1'2   24 INCHES

Grace Dieu:

Watercolour by Michael Prynne, one of the 1930s team which investigated Grace Dieu. It shows a cross-section through a fragment of a frame and outer planking. This makes clear the complex construction. Each run of planking, called a strake, is made up of three securely fastened layers of planks. The ship was built up from the keel, strake upon strake. These are held together by iron nails driven from inboard. Outboard their ends are turned down, clenched, over a washer-like rove. As the planking rose, frames (ribs) were progressively inserted. Their outboard faces were notched (joggled) to fit over the steps in the planking and its fastenings. Planks and frames were fastened together by treenails, large wooden dowels which passed through all the layers.

Plate 3

Unusual artefacts from sixteenth-century shipwrecks.

Top: Bartholomew Ledge. Surviving specimens from a cargo of deliberately broken bells.

Bottom: St Anthony. Painted panels of saints in a church near the wreck site are of a style and date which suggest they were salvaged from the ship in 1527.

Plate 4

Above: blue & manganese-purple painted plates made in Seville graced the tables of the New World settlement, La Isabela, founded by Columbus in January 1494 and abandoned four years later.

Below: like the Iberian ships that pioneered the Atlantic crossing, the Studland Bay Wreck was carrying Isabela polychrome pottery.

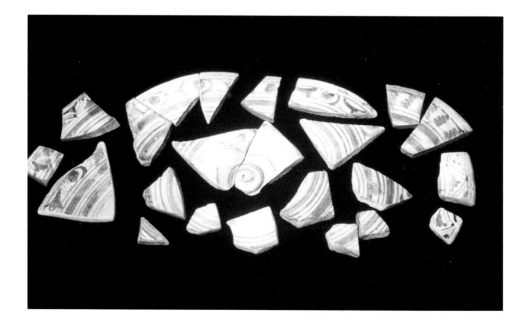

Plate 5

A

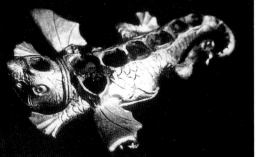

C

B

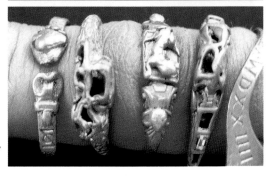

F

D

Girona:

A   *Divers controlling the ascent of a bronze esmeril 1.63m long, using two air-bags.*

B   *Talisman against fire, a pendant in the form of a salamander; gold and rubies.*

C   *A few of the 414 gold coins from the wreck with spherical gold buttons from a tunic, pendants and links from a chain.*

D   *Link of an elaborate chain set with a ruby and two pearls.*

E   *Ready money: a heavy gold chain 1.22m (4ft) long, as worn by Spanish grandees, with links which could be detached to pay for goods or services in time of need.*

F   *Five rings: hand holding a heart and inscribed 'I have nothing more to give thee'; crushed ring with empty settings; ring with a salamander in relief flanked by heads; crushed ring with two diamonds remaining; large ring inscribed 'Madame de Champigny MDXXIIII' and worn by her grandson on Girona.*

E

Plate 6

Church Rocks:

Top: a bronze weight from the end of a steelyard. The measurement of rations and other commodities was an essential chore in seafaring.

Centre: a merchant's brand or seal.

Bottom: a sherd of Ming porcelain brought from the other side of the world. Chinese porcelain has been found on other Armada-period ships.

Plate 7

Amsterdam:
Top: group of exceptionally well-preserved finds includes a lead-lined barrel filled with a tallowy substance, bottles of wine, drinking glasses, cutlery and footwear. Left: silk flower from a textile (on a copper wire frame). Right: leather cartridge cases.

Plate 8

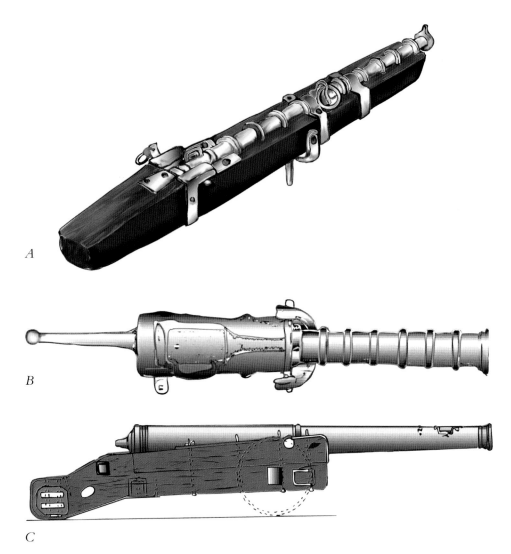

A

B

C

Guns From the Sea:

A   *Early sixteenth-century 'tube gun' made from a wrought-iron tube reinforced with rings and fitted in a wooden bed. This enabled the separate firing chamber to be wedged tightly in position. To take aim the gun was swivelled on its yoke and the touch hole in the chamber was lit with a taper. The Cattewater swivel guns were 2m (6.5ft) long overall and had a bore of 55mm (2.2in).*

B   *The Tal-y-Bont wreck showed that wrought-iron swivel guns continued in use up to the eighteenth century. The design improved. Aiming was by means of a tiller and the chamber was wedged in an integral holder. Typical length was 1.30m (4.25ft) with a bore of 50mm (2in).*

C   *Late sixteenth-century bronze minion on an iron-bound carriage. The Church Rocks gun was 3.6m (10ft 11in) long overall with a bore of 76mm (3in) and was cast in Venice.*

Plate 9

D   *Bronze saker from Dunwich Bank.*
     Cast in Flanders for the Emperor of
     Germany between 1536 and
     1556, it is 3.38m (10.3ft) long
     and has a bore of 95mm (3.75in).

E   *Cast-iron finbanker from the Erme*
     Estuary site. It is marked XXI
     denoting its calibre in Swedish pounds
     and measures 2.69m (8.6ft) in length
     with a bore of 90mm (3.5in). It may
     have been cast as late as 1720.

Plate 10

Mary:

Personal possessions of wealthy passengers. Top: a ring with an octagonal bezel and unidentified coat of arms. Left: delicately enamelled ring with settings for table and rose cut diamonds. Right: silver earring, probably worn by a man, set with seven glass or quartz stones. Bottom: 'memento mori' lockets of gold filigree and enamel containing strands of human hair.

Plate 11

The Pwll Fanog
Historic Wreck:
Top: aerial view of the Menai Strait with Anglesey on the left. The wreck site lies ahead of the moving boat.

Centre: reconstruction by Owain Roberts of the clinker-built coaster with a single squaresail.

Below: stacked slates of the cargo mound colonised by Dead Men's Fingers (Alcyonium digitatum).

Plate 12

The challenge of taking archaeology underwater. Simple tasks on land tax the most experienced diver and archaeologist on the seabed. Top: fixing datum points on the rocky bottom of the Coronation site is a physical, oxygen-demanding task. Bottom: the currents on the Tal-y-Bont site make a long tape-measure difficult to manage.

Plate 13

Stirling Castle:
Top: two navigation slates. These were used for recording course and wind direction.
Centre: navigational dividers, brass buckles and buttons.
Bottom: marine's leather hat. The lighter leather of the crown is modern.

Plate 14

Invincible:
Top: solid oak plate as issued to the crew, giving rise to the phrase 'a square meal'. Brandy bottle, stave-built tankard for grog or beer, and spoons of pewter and wood. Bottom: a child's shoe, woollen sock and very early regimental buttons.

Plate 15

Reconstruction by the British Museum of a Greek tomb in southern Italy. The dead man has his prized possessions around him, including a wine-mixing bowl, pitchers and cups. Such tombs were the source of William Hamilton's First Collection of 'vases' which were bought by the British Museum. While these have been on view to the public for two centuries, eight cases of his Second Collection were lost aboard Colossus. *The British Museum paid for the recovery of thousands of sherds from the wreck site.*

Plate 16

Contemporary painting of the dramatic moment when Pomone *struck the Needles. Distress rockets scream into the air from the dismasted ship.*

Contour map of the Pomone *wreck site plotted in 1997 by Submetrix Ltd using ISIS100. The yellow and greens show the changing, though shallow, depths over the fissured chalk seabed. The green, through turquoise to dark blue, is the slope into deep water on the north side of the Needles lighthouse. Red areas were outside the swathe of the survey which can read to the very edge of the water.*

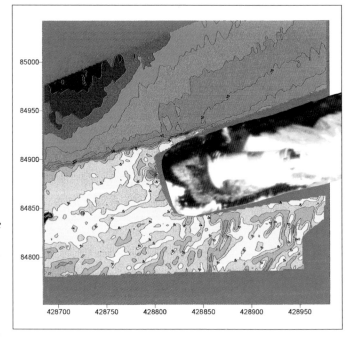

and glimpsed a white object on the seabed. It was a lead ingot. Soon afterwards he saw two green-grey tubes which he recognised as a bronze saker and an esmeril; *Girona* had been found.

Two years and 6000 diving hours later his team had recovered about 10,000 objects. From the old records Robert Stenuit knew that these had come from three Armada vessels, *Girona* plus the two abandoned ships. In the high-energy zone round the rocks there were hardly any traces of the ship itself: only some nails; lead sheeting and ballast; and tiny fragments of rope. All but two of her guns and one of her anchors appeared to have been already cast overboard. Some navigational equipment was found: dividers and two sea-worn astrolabes.

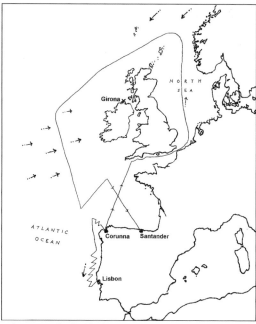

The Armada fled before the wind into the North Sea with orders to return home. At least 63 vessels were lost, 20 on the coast of Ireland.

Girona was a treasure-hunter's dream: the officers and gentlemen had with them stylish silver and pewter tableware, and the finery which they planned to show off in conquered England. More than 1000 gold and silver coins, heavy gold chains and a superb collection of gold and gem-set jewellery were recovered. However, for Robert Stenuit the reward for his years of research was to be able to identify the original owners of many of the pieces. A red-enamelled gold cross had belonged to Don Alonso de Leiva, the second in command of the Armada. After being injured in the wrecking of his ship he had to be carried 32km (20 miles) to join *Girona*. Her captain was probably the owner of the white-enamelled Order of St John. One ring dated 1524 could be traced to the grandmother of a young man on board. Bringing home the impact of the tragedy for those at home in Spain was another ring, a hand clasping a heart and the inscription *No tengo mas que dar te* ('I have nothing more to give thee'). Voyages of exploration had brought this wealth to Spain. The gold had almost certainly come from the New World and the diamonds, rubies, lapis lazuli and pearls from Asia.

Stenuit's team were determined that the material should not be dispersed at public auction. After two years of legal negotiations and a public appeal all the artefacts were acquired by Ulster Museum where they are superbly displayed, 'a triumph for the museum and a tribute to the finder'. Designated in 1992, it is the only wreck in Northern Ireland to be protected under the Act.

Display: Ulster Museum; information in the Giant's Causeway interpretation centre
Further reading: Stenuit, R. 1974. *Treasures of the Armada*; Flanagan, L. 1988. *Ireland's Armada Legacy* (catalogue)
Viewpoint: The National Trust maintain the footpath past the Giant's Causeway and Lacada Point

Church Rocks (see Colour Plate 6)
Teignmouth, Devon

General Location: SX 9472 7322

Protection: 50° 32.92'N 03° 29.17'W, 200 yards square
ARCHAEOLOGICAL

Armament: includes bronze cannon and swivel guns

Lost: probably late 16th century

A holiday resort is the location of a shipwreck found in 1975. No-one knew it existed although it lay only 150m off the beach. Its contents bear a close resemblance to those on Armada wrecks in Ireland and Scotland.

Simon Burton was only thirteen and snorkelling over Church Rocks when he saw a large green tube protruding from the sand about 7m below. He soon realised that it was a cannon. Despite his excitement he did what the most experienced diver would have done, surfaced to look for landmarks so that he could find it again. Simon's father, Philip, enlisted a local boatman to recover the cannon and, against advice, was convinced that there were more to find. Their venture into shipwreck exploration put them on a rapid learning curve in the logistics of seabed work and recovery, the law of salvage and the practice of archaeology.

Despite searching no more cannon were found. Then, in 1977, Simon found cannon balls and a swivel gun. Despite this, their request for the site to be protected was turned down on the grounds that there was insufficient information. The seabed was dropping, possibly as a result of new beach groynes starving the site of sand. A second cannon appeared, this time attached to the remains of a wooden carriage. Raising it seemed the best safeguard and route to information. To everyone's dismay, the lift by a fishing boat went wrong when swell shifted the cannon and broke the carriage. Margaret Rule from the *Mary Rose* and Alex Flinder from BSAC then visited and the site was protected by an emergency designation.

Designation set parameters for the investigation: survey was permitted but for the time being no more lifts. Unfortunately the Protection of Wrecks Act was only framed to stop unauthorised interference in wreck sites and its clauses included no provision to assist investigating teams with funds, equipment or professional help. When the Receiver of Wreck sold the first cannon the generous salvage award to the Burtons was ploughed back, to purchase a boat for the dive team. The Church Rocks project, like many other designated sites, was continued on a shoe-string budget by enthusiasts applying their diverse skills and ingenuity to the logistical problems of the seabed. At times the requirements of archaeological licences seem an added burden. In 1983 Simon Burton felt he could no longer make the commitment of time, effort and money.

After seven years the wreck was left unidentified and dormant despite the very special finds. By this time 6 bronze guns had been lifted: an elegant saker purchased by English Heritage and displayed at Pendennis Castle; 2 smaller minions; and 3 swivel guns complete with their iron breech blocks, wedges, swivels and chains, one of which the Tower of London Armouries bought. For both the cannon and the swivel guns the only parallels come from *La Trinidad Valencera*, an Armada ship wrecked in Ireland. The cannon were made by Sigismundo Alberghetti II. He was master gunfounder in the prestigious Venice works from 1582-1601, and had worked previously in Florence. A steelyard weight, made of copper alloy and filled with lead, again matches examples found on *Girona* and *La Trinidad Valencera*, as does a large copper cooking kettle found along with bones of sheep, cattle and chicken.

Historians may refute that this is a 1588 Armada ship. There are other options, as Philip II sent further armadas during his war with England. These were similarly dispersed by the weather with some ships driven ashore or missing. *La Trinidad Valencera* has provided the best match for Church Rocks artefacts. She was a Venetian merchantman taken into Spanish control. It is possible that Church Rocks was an armed ship trading between Venice and southern Britain. Such a vessel was wrecked on the Shingles, Isle of Wight, in 1587. By coincidence, the only other seabed discovery of an Alberghetti minion was made just 150m from the nearby Yarmouth Roads Wreck.

Work on the Church Rocks site was resumed in 1990 under the auspices of Teignmouth Museum. There is now 1-2m (3-6ft) of mobile sand over the area and a recently constructed storm water outfall has deposited red clay particles. However, excavation has enabled a 1:10 drawing to be made of the only piece of surviving ship structure so far found. This measures 7.3m by 1.2m (24 x 4ft) and appears to be part of the stern and lower starboard hull. The planking is carvel but, like the Studland Bay Wreck, there is no trace of caulking.

Sadly, the frenetic treatment of the site by Channel 4's Time Team in 1995 was no substitute for long-term resources, the lack of which continues to limit results.

Ceramic firepot from Church Rocks similar to those found on Armada wrecks. It was thrown aboard enemy ships where the burning fuses tied around the outside would ignite the gunpowder, spirits and resin as it broke on the deck.

Viewpoint: to the east of the
Teignmouth Corinthian Yacht Club there is a wreck notice on the seawall promenade
Display: Burton Room, Teignmouth Museum
Further reading: Wilson, V. 1993. *Burton's Bounty. The Story of Teignmouth's Mysterious Wreck*; Preece, C. & Burton, S, 1993. Church Rocks, 1975-83: a reassessment. *International Journal of Nautical Archaeology*, 22.3: 257-66

Dunwich Bank
Dunwich, Suffolk

General Location: TM 490 685
Protection: 52° 15.14'N 01° 38.53'E, 100m radius
          ARCHAEOLOGICAL
Lost: probably after 1551

The search for 1588 wrecks always sparks interest because, from childhood, the Spanish Armada is strongly imprinted in our shared historical memory. Many sea battles of equal national importance are now only remembered by historians, but some still hold the imaginations of the communities which were closest to the action. One such is the Battle of Sole Bay in May 1672, when the Dutch swept down on the Anglo-French fleet anchored off the Suffolk coast. The burning and sinking of the 104-gun *Royal James* is part of Dunwich's history and has inspired hardy wreck hunters for decades. It is a strange twist of fate that their most promising discovery now seems more likely to be linked with the Armada period.

A permanent exhibition opened by Stuart Bacon in Orford explains the work of the Suffolk Underwater Unit. Volunteers have monitored the changing coast and recorded ship remains brought up by fishermen or washed onto the beaches. A major project has mapped the remains of the prosperous city of medieval Dunwich which now lie on the seabed. Their work confirms that many metres of land are lost each year and that shipwrecks now found on Dunwich Bank were actually lost close to the old shoreline.

Stuart Bacon joined forces with George Spence and other divers hunting the *Royal James*. Whenever finances or sponsorship made it possible they employed vessels to conduct remote sensing surveys. It was during one of these surveys in 1994 that a single bronze gun was found and lifted. Unlike Church Rocks the site was rapidly designated.

The cannon lay on sand and shingle among concretion mounds but exploration is painfully slow as there is usually zero visibility in the sediment-filled waters. Everything is achieved by touch, with knotted lines and hand-spans replacing tape measures. A rare spell of clear water coincided with a visit of the Archaeological Diving Unit. With their surface demand breathing apparatus, communications and video equipment they rapidly recorded a second gun where it lay on the seabed.

Shell UK have supported the local diving team, and promised funds for 1998. Stuart Bacon and George Spence, however, know that the wreck can only be effectively investigated by a fully equipped and financed professional team. With little precedent for the necessary funding being available through heritage agencies they have begun looking at the options for cooperation with commercial salvage companies. In 1997 this project planning was taking place while a commercial salvage operation in Cornwall provoked the designation of *Hanover* as a Historic Wreck. It has yet to be seen what structure the Dunwich project will take and how it might operate under the Protection of Wrecks Act.

Meanwhile the seabed tally has risen to five bronze and four heavily concreted iron guns. Two bronze guns have been successfully researched. The conclusion is complex and based on the worn mouldings of the first gun and its dimensions which correspond to Spanish feet. It was cast at Malines in the Spanish Netherlands by a famous founder called Remigny de Halut. However, he used a design produced by a German founder, Loffler. Study of surviving guns, the ordnance requirements of various European monarchs and the order books of gunfounders suggest that it was made between 1536 and 1556. The wear inside the gun indicates that it had been in use for at least a couple of decades. It seems that the two guns would not have been out of place on an Armada period ship. Indeed, it is actually guns on *La Trinidad Valencera* which show that de Halut was using Loffler designs.

SUFFOLK UNDERWATER STUDIES

DATE:	2.6.1994		Grid Ref:	685
FIND NO	675		LOG ENTRY	
DESCRIPTION OF FIND AND MATERIAL		Bronze Demi Culverin 11 foot(3.3528)m Almost 2 tons		
CONDITION		Crest and dolpins eroded by shingle and sand friction		
COMMENTS		The first major find on the Dunwich Bank wreck site		
DATE RECOVERED + FINDER		2.6.1994 Stuart R Bacon		
PHOTO NO.				
TREATMENT + DATE				

The cannon was immersed in a purpose built tank filled with salt water, then into fresh water, pumped through the bore. Followed by stabalisation in sodium bicarbonate.
Tank built by Sparrows of Nuclear Electric, Sizewell.

A small fragment of wood was originally attached to the side of the gun, near the RH trunnion, looking from the breach.

Photo: after cleaning at Sizewell.

Record sheets are used to record any objects which are reported to the Suffolk Underwater Unit by divers fishermen or beachwalkers.

Liaison with a dredging company enabled Stuart Bacon to study timbers pulled from the seabed. Behind him is the toothed cutting-head of the dredger.

Display: Orford Crafts for both the raised gun and information on Suffolk underwater archaeology
Further reading: Bacon, S. *Southwold, Suffolk*, 44-93; Roth, R. 1996. The cannon from Dunwich Bank, Suffolk. *International Journal of Nautical Archaeology*, 25.1: 21-32
Viewpoint: the site is immediately offshore from the Visitor's Centre at Dunwich Heath Nature Reserve where there is a viewing gallery

Rhinns of Islay
Islay, Strathclyde

General Location: NR 1536 5401
Protection: REVOKED 55° 41′ 45″N 06° 31′ 50″W, 100m radius

ARCHAEOLOGICAL

Multiple Wreck Site

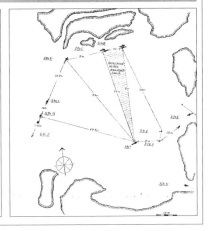

Girona, and *La Trinidad Valencera* were discoveries to excite the least historically minded divers. It was the story of a 1588 Armada wreck which brought the RAF London SAC to one of the most forbidding and remote dive sites imaginable: Frenchman's Rocks.

Their search was inspired by Lord Burghley's report to Elizabeth I that the Lord of the Scottish Isles had written to inform her of a great Spanish ship being wrecked. Their researcher Mike Cameron concluded that he was referring to one of four Armada ships which were presumed lost after rounding Scotland. Using old maps he focused on Orsay, just off the coast of Islay and with the help of local lore narrowed the search to Frenchman's Rocks off the Rhinns of Islay.

When the diving team arrived in 1975 they saw 'an evil little reef if ever there was one'. The Rocks consist of nine islets swept clean by the pounding Atlantic waves and south westerly gales. The first dive was made with great caution but, among the rocks, proved tolerable, with a strong surge from the swell the main problem. This could hurl a diver

Viewpoint: average conditions on Frenchman's Rocks, the offshore and inaccessible site. Sheets of spray are thrown up by waves hitting the seaward rocks and there is the awesome noise of an 8-knot tide race rushing past on either side.

5m (16ft) in each direction. The true fearfulness of the site was experienced in 1977. Huge breakers held up diving for days and a team tried to start work in a brief respite: 'the horrifying residual surge literally hurled them to the surface from 12m'.

In 1975 the defiance of conditions had paid off with the divers locating four heavily concreted guns and the site was designated. In the following season some of the rock gullies previously filled with shingle had been swept clear to a depth of about 12m (39ft). Here a range of objects were found but proved more useful as demonstrations of local sea conditions than as positive clues to the wreck's identity.

The finds included cannon balls so worn away that they appeared as flat discs in the surface of concretions. This also contained lead shot and bar shot. Four pot-like iron objects initially defied identification until it was realised that they were the eroded stumps of some form of swivel gun. Other objects still embedded in concretion were described as 'toilet seat' shape but believed to be cannon lying at an angle and, in effect, sliced down by erosion to the level of the concretion. The truth of the theory was proved when trial excavation was licensed in 1977. The side of one gun protected by concretion showed reinforcing rings, touch hole and a cascabel, unusually square in shape. The trial excavation also found objects other than ordnance. These included glass and some small pieces of gold and silver thought to come from the handles of items such as cutlery and pistols.

The team laboured tirelessly at hand excavation of the concretions and even tried out their own design of underwater pneumatic drill. This proved rather hazardous and hopes were pinned on using small explosive charges in future seasons. Archaeologists had successfully used explosives on *Adelaar* in the Outer Hebrides.

The identity of the site was never proven and the destructive force of the sea had left nothing to rival the artefacts from the known Armada wrecks. In 1978 the discovery of a two reale coin dated 1788, some early nineteenth-century brass buttons and an eighteenth-century style mortar all pointed to it actually being the site of more than one wreck. The name of the Rocks is after all reminiscent of the French man-of-war which local legend recounts as sinking there. The presence of metal wrecks, such as the *Blytheville* and several trawlers, confirm that the rocks are a multiple wreck location.

In 1984 the designation of the Historic Wreck was revoked: 'the Secretary of State being of the opinion that there is no longer any wreck there which requires protecting'.

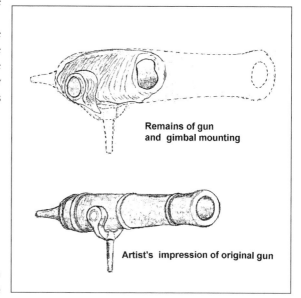

Remains of gun and gimbal mounting

Interpretation of the remains of a swivel gun.

Artist's impression of original gun

Collections: Islay Museum Trust has a few of the objects from the wreck site

Coins and Measures

As international trade developed the lack of standardisation of measurement made huge complications. Cargo manifests had to state the national unit being used, for instance, peso de Castilia, peso de Sicilia. *Girona* was carrying gunpowder: 200 Neapolitan pounds (891g) and 208 Castilian pounds (460g). In Spain pounds varied from 345g in Avila, to 460g in Castile, and 575g in Corunna. It is, therefore, hardly surprising that weights and balances are found on many historic shipwrecks.

Guns were cast and ships built to national units, but the 'feet' used were different. While matching the dimensions of a gun with one of these units can help to identify its nationality, the fragmented remains of hull structure are more difficult to compare directly with historically documented measurements.

A few coins cannot be used to identify the nationality or even the last voyage of a shipwreck. On *Girona* 1325 coins have been found, 414 gold, 789 silver and 122 base metal. They come from mints in six countries. They are a large and very important group with which finds from less precisely dated shipwrecks can be compared.

Gold jewellery on *Girona* was almost certainly made from New World gold. By the mid-sixteenth century more than four tons were crossing the Atlantic each year, about six times what was being brought from the Gold Coast by its main exploiters, the Portuguese.

New World silver cast in 'pieces of eight' and other denominations became de facto an international currency and could be stored or hoarded for years. Pieces minted as much as a century before Clowdisley Shovell's fleet hit the Scillies in 1707 were found in the wrecks of his ships. European ships took large quantities of this silver to the Far East to trade for porcelain, spices, tea and silks.

6 Outward Bound for the Indies

Bland food, dull earthenware and boring old woollens and tweeds sums up English living before adventurers brought back spices, dyes, fine porcelain, silks and patterned cottons from the Indian and China seas. Any sixteenth-century merchant could see the market for such exotic goods but no individual could raise the capital to send ships to the other side of the world. Portugal, England, Holland, France, Denmark and Sweden formed East India Companies. Their organisation was monumental. For the English company alone, despite the destruction of 323 tons of records, there are still 14.5km (9 miles) of shelving holding its ledgers.

The Dutch East India Company (VOC) was founded in 1602. It had 250 trading stations throughout Asia, ranging from a Company representative working with local staff to garrisoned settlements. There were 35,000 personnel in Asia. The annual fleets carried money to pay these staff and purchase goods. During two centuries the VOC built 1700 vessels and 5000 ship movements are recorded between Holland and Asia, with 3300 ships making the return journey.

Wrecks of East Indiamen are spread along the route from the English Channel, to the Cape of Good Hope and across the Indian Ocean and beyond the Malaysian Archipelego. About 220 English and 246 Dutch ships are known to have been lost.

With outward cargoes of copper and silver and homeward cargoes such as porcelain, the wrecks are honeypots for commercial salvors. The detailed archives help treasure hunters to identify the richest cargoes, locate the wreck sites and authenticate the recovered material. Paradoxically it is the same interaction between historical records and artefacts which makes East India shipwrecks such important archaeological sites.

Kennemerland
Outer Skerries, Shetland

General Location: HU 688 713
Protection: 60° 25.20'N 00° 45.00'W, 250m radius

HISTORICAL

Built: 1661
Type: Dutch (VOC) East Indiaman
Dimensions: 155 x 35ft (47.3x10.7m)
Armament: included 24 iron and 6 bronze guns
Lost: 20 December 1664
Voyage: Amsterdam to Batavia   **Cargo:** wine; silver; cloth; mercury; lead

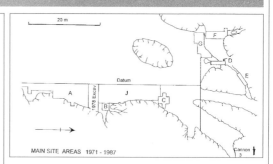

MAIN SITE AREAS 1971 - 1987

Today, with engines, reliable charts and well-marked hazards, ships use more direct routes than was possible in the age of sail. Then long detours might be taken to pick up a following wind or to avoid pirates and privateers. For the highly successful Dutch East India Company (VOC) the first leg of the 12,000-mile voyage to Asia was most dangerous. Rather than risk the English Channel Dutch merchantmen loaded with bullion and European luxuries often chose the 'achter om' route north round Scotland.

On 14 December 1664 *Kennemerland* and *Rijnland* left Texel for Batavia with a general cargo and 240,000 guilders. Six days later *Kennemerland* was wrecked on Stoura Stack, a rock pinnacle in the entrance of the Out Skerries natural harbour. She broke in two. Her mast touched the stack enabling her pilot and two seamen to scramble to safety. The bow drove into the harbour and was cast up on Bruray Island, though much of the wreckage washed out to sea on the next tide. Shetlanders remember her as '*Carmelan*' in a rhyme descibing the accident. Charles II claimed the salvaged goods including the silver.

The first sign of *Kennemerland* were cannon near Stoura Stack found by divers working on another East Indiaman, *De Liefde*. Zetland Council had already recognised the importance of maritime heritage and held seabed leases to protect a few of the many documented shipwrecks around their 4800km (3000 miles) of coastline. Therefore, Zetland Museum was closely involved from 1971 when student divers from Aston University took up the search of the *Kennemerland* area. Over many seasons the site became a test-bed for first-class underwater archaeological recording. It was used to demonstrate analytical methods for scattered wreck sites, and produced some exceptional objects.

The search was widened to cover not only Stoura Stack but the harbour bottom as far as the surf zone around Bruray Island. The kelp-covered, boulder-strewn bed seemed unpromising for preservation but artefacts were found within a gravel layer. A few gullies had sufficient depth to contain more rich deposits, though divers recorded the destructive effect of burrowing crabs on apparently secure stratigraphy. Excavation was confined to gullies, while survey focused on determining the horizontal relationships across the whole site.

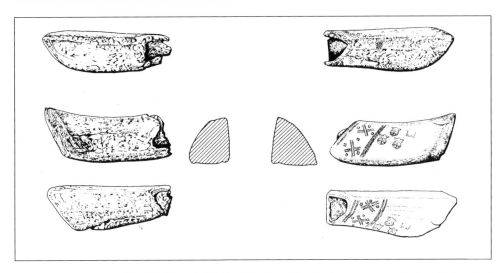

For six years a group of small objects defied identification. Finally they were recognised as the heads of golf clubs from which the shafts had broken or decayed. They were formed from a core of wood with a lead casing. A shipwreck is an unlikely source of information on the early history of golf. However, the game became a craze in seventeenth-century Holland and Kennemerland's passengers will have been planning to play it in Batavia.

The initial impact and breaking of the ship on Stoura Stack was apparent from the concentration of guns, lead ingots and bricks. A second group of bricks opposite Grunday indicated another impact in the surf zone, while guns further into the harbour suggest part of the buoyant wreckage was driven onwards. The distribution of artefacts across the whole site was mapped on a theoretical grid of 1m squares. Keith Muckelroy divided the many individual objects into categories which might appear on post-medieval wreck sites, for example green bottle-glass fragments, bronze nails and lead fragments. He used the data to begin testing the validity of using statistical analyses to interpret the break up of a ship and dispersal of its contents. This approach fuelled survey and artefact analysis for *Assurance/Pomone*.

Excavation included some arduous tasks such as raising, weighing, drawing and recording all 119 lead ingots. England was Holland's major supplier of lead and the ingots are a source of information on the industry which is not otherwise available. Their date stamps also confirm the wreck as *Kennemerland*. The importance of metals is clear from the mercury found inside a stoneware jug in which it was being transshipped to Batavia, probably for the refining of gold. Fruit stones show that ceramic and glass containers were being used to transport peaches and plums, undoubtedly preserved in syrup or alcohol. Concretions brought ashore for excavation produced more organic material, barley husks and peppercorns.

Viewpoint: the ferry to the Skerries passes over the site on its way into the harbour
Collections: Shetland Museum, Lerwick
Further reading: Dobbs, C. & Price, R. The *Kennemerland* site. An interim report. The sixth and seventh seasons, 1984 & 1987, and the identification of five golf clubs. *International Journal of Nautical Archaeology*, 20.2: 111-22

Amsterdam
Bulverhythe, East Sussex

General Location: TQ 778 083   **Protection:** 50° 50' 42"N 00° 31' 39"E, 100m radius

HISTORICAL

Built: 1747

Type: Dutch East Indiaman

Dimensions: 150 x 35ft

(45.7x10.7m)

Armament: 54 guns

Lost: 26 January 1749

Voyage: Texel to Batavia

Cargo: general goods

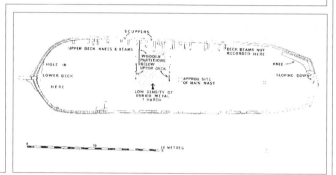

The largely intact hull of the *Amsterdam* is cradled nearly upright in the soft beach. At the lowest tides her outline is clear and her stempost still points shorewards. She was a brand-new armed merchantman built in four months to an improved specification by the VOC and was en route to Batavia.

Company records detail her dimensions, the number of seamen, soldiers and passengers on board and her cargo. This included French wine, silver lace and other fine clothing for the ex-patriates. To pay for a return cargo she carried 24 chests of silver bars and 4 chests containing 16,000 silver ducatoons. In Asia the silver commanded a higher price than gold.

In many cases the cause of a wreck can only be guessed. The short voyage of *Amsterdam*, like the long voyage of *Girona*, is documented and gives meaning to the phrases 'adverse weather' and 'blown off course'. They show how in the age of sail contrary winds could delay departure for weeks, drive ships in the wrong direction and wear out a crew made ill by food and water which had turned foul.

On 4 November 1748 *Amsterdam* left Texel for a 12,000-mile voyage, but had to anchor for four days when the wind turned to the north-west. She put back into Texel and made a second attempt on the 21st, only to spend another two weeks battling to make headway. She returned to the shelter of Texel and storms kept her there until 8 January when she finally set off, crossing the North Sea in one day – only to run into a terrible south-west gale. For twelve days her captain struggled to ride out the gale as 50 men died and 40 became seriously ill, reducing the number available to sail the ship. *Amsterdam* headed for the shelter of Pevensey Bay, but grounded and her rudder was ripped off. Now she was in serious trouble. Anchors were let go and held, but two days later the cables parted. With a crew that had drowned their sorrow with alcohol she fired distress signals but no help came.

Then her luck changed. Instead of being smashed to pieces in the surf, she ran aground on the soft silt of a former river mouth. The survivors got ashore and, guarded by soldiers, twenty seven chests of money were carried to Hastings Customs House. The sand engulfed her so rapidly that local people were unable to reach her cargo and the Company had to abandon its efforts at salvage the following year. She became buried to her upper deck.

Amsterdam is by far the most complete of some 30 located East Indiamen. Her position on the beach was always known but disregarded until, in 1969, workmen building a sewer nearby used their mechanical excavator to dig into the middle of the ship and recovered 5 bronze guns still wrapped in their sacking plus a wonderful assortment of beautifully preserved objects and ship's fittings. Much of the material was dispersed; two of the cannon disappeared and bottles of wine were said to have been sold for a few pounds in local bars. In his spare time Peter Marsden tracked down, analysed and drew all the items he could find and organised an Anglo-Dutch survey of the remains.

The site was designated in 1974 and the following year the Dutch Government as legal heirs of the Company claimed ownership and set up the Stichting VOC-Schip Amsterdam to initiate research and excavation. There followed plans to raise and return the wreck to Amsterdam. These did not gain momentum and instead a programme of limited investigation over several seasons took place. This aimed to develop excavation techniques and combine archaeological and historical information in one database. Such an integrated approach would produce a greater understanding of the construction of the vessel and of all aspects of the Company.

Excavation at the stern of the ship revealed its carved decoration, and the contents of the gunroom on the lower deck with the surgeon's medicine chest. A tub still containing fat confirmed the exceptional survival of materials.

The enormity of raising the ship was also brought home and no further fieldwork was undertaken for seven years. During that time the iron excavation scaffold erected beyond the stern seems to have caused scouring, and exposed portions of the hull are visibly deteriorating. In 1996 a three-year collaborative study began to record the hull, with geophysical, biological and topographical survey. The erection of a groin within 100m of the designated area has highlighted the importance of monitoring sediment transport.

Viewpoint: an interpretation panel now marks Amsterdam *damaged in 1969.*

Display: Hastings Shipwreck Heritage Centre
Further reading: Marsden, P. 1985. *The Wreck of the Amsterdam*

South Edinburgh Channel
Thames Estuary, Kent

General Location: TR 2526 8616
Protection: 51° 31.73′N 01° 14.88′E,
100m radius
ARCHAEOLOGICAL
Dimension: 35 x 15m (115 x 49ft)
estimated remains
Lost: probably late eighteenth century
Cargo: Swedish copper plate 'money';
iron bars and luxury goods
In the eighteenth century, as old charts show, the Long Sand formed a huge obstacle to shipping.

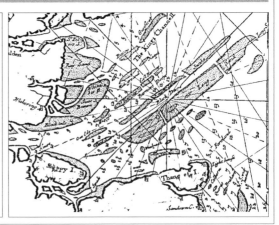

Historic Wreck sites in Britain were classified by the archaeologist, Keith Muckelroy, in 1977. In his Class 1, the most coherent wrecks, he included *Mary Rose* and *Amsterdam* together with an unpublicised wreck in the Thames Estuary.

In autumn 1972 during a main survey of the South Edinburgh Channel, the wreck was first charted by the Port of London Authority (PLA). Over five years the channel moved 400m westward. By 1974 the wreck was exposed to a height of 6m (20ft) on the north-eastern side of the North Shingles Bank. It was thus only 50 - 100m west of the shipping channel and expected to become a navigational hazard. A sonar sweep by the survey vessel *Maplin* in March 1975 recorded the wreck as about 40m long and the top only 2.4m (8ft) below low water. However, charted movement of the channel showed that the ship could not have sailed to its position within the last 150 years.

The PLA made a detailed sonar survey and requested the National Maritime Museum to send an observer while they dived on the site. Peter Van der Merwe visited and advised the clearance divers in making a sketch map and lifting sample items from the ship. Visibility ranged from zero to 18m. The exposed hull had a mid-section 15 - 20m (49 - 66 ft) in length and rested on a plateau of hard sand with at least one deck on the east side. Collapsed spars and structure included three iron cannon (one had a bore of about 10cm (4in) and was protruding through a port), stanchions and knees.

The hold was filled with Swedish copper plate 'money' stacked in blocks at the north end. Spanning the width of the hold was a cargo of iron anchors, about 1.8m (6ft) from fluke to fluke, in four tiers of three, lying on a stout transverse beam. In the centre were iron bars 8 - 10cm (3 - 4in) wide and 2.4 - 3m (8 - 10ft) long in bales with stacked sheet glass to the west. Beyond this was a cargo of crates of bottles in two sizes, still corked and full of red wine, and also square brown bottles. In addition the divers reported luxury items, wheel-cut glass goblets and tumblers and 'smooth dishes in a bale' and recovered sherds of a Wedgwood pearlware tureen. In some concretion an Indian Ocean cowrie shell was later found.

The 'best fit' for this wreck is an unidentified large sailing ship, flying the Swedish flag, noted in *Lloyds List*, as wrecked on Long Sands on 16 October 1787. In 1777 plate money ceased to be legal tender and the Bank of Sweden disposed of its reserves simply as copper until about 1800. Records show that betrween 1781 and 1800 an average of 40 tons of copper plates were exported annually. It is possible that the South Edinburgh Channel Wreck was carrying the total for one year. For Swedish numismatists and archaeologists the site is of the highest importance; no other finds of Swedish copper and iron cargoes are known from this period.

Cowrie shells were used as currency in parts of the Far East and have been found on the site of the *Svecia* wrecked on the Orkneys in 1740. She was a Swedish East Indiaman homeward bound from Bengal with a cargo of silks and cotton. Perhaps the South Edinburgh Channel ship was bound directly for the Indies with European luxuries for the table as well as metals and window glass. As a match has yet to be found in Swedish records Dr Cederlund of Stockholm University suggests she was one of the large Swedish merchantmen taking goods to London for onward shipment to the Indies.

Sadly, the exceptionally intact hulls of *Stirling Castle* and South Edinburgh Channel lacked the kind of rapid professional response in recording and subsequent monitoring which on land is funded for sites of key importance. The channel is not due to be surveyed again until 2006.

Right: a piece of Swedish plate money with 2-'daler' stamps.

Below: display in Gdansk Maritime Museum of baled iron bars and circular copper plates recovered from a 16th-century Baltic wreck.

Viewpoint: the wreck lies 16km (10 miles) from the nearest land and the South Edinburgh Channel itself is now shoaling

Collections: National Maritime Museum

Admiral Gardner
Goodwin Sands, Kent

General Location: TR 4513 5044
Protection: 51° 12.00'N 01° 30.56'E,
150m radius
HISTORICAL
Built: 1797
Type: English East Indiaman
Dimensions: 145 x 36ft (44.2 x 11m)
Armament: 32 guns
Lost: 25 January 1809
Voyage: London to Madras
Cargo: iron goods; copper
Complement: 168 crew

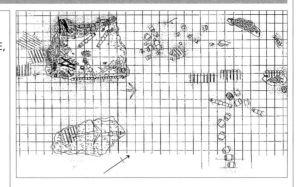

In August 1806 the new East India Dock was opened. Two ships ceremonially entered: *City of London*, whose name honoured the trading capital of the world; and the nine-year-old *Admiral Gardner* which was being honoured for her action against the 44-gun *Bellona*, a reminder that East Indiamen were equal to ships-of-the-line.

Enclosed docks were proposed to counter congestion, danger and theft. Ships lay afloat in locked basins while off-loading into dock-side warehouses was carefully regulated. London's dock-building heyday was initiated by Acts of Parliament in 1799. Private companies recouped their investment on construction by charging docking fees and, for ease of administration, docks were divided by origin of cargo.

The East India Dock was built at downstream Blackwall where Indiamen, too large to easily reach the Pool of London, had traditionally offloaded. It was unusual in serving only the ships of the East India Company, which still held a monopoly, and in having no warehouses. The Company retained its warehouses in the heart of the City and built Commercial Road to link these with the new dock. With an adjoining fitting-out basin, the dock was used to care for the ships. Many arrived in perilous condition. To keep them afloat teams of labourers, as many as 60 per ship, often worked their pumps continuously.

In 1809 the veteran *Admiral Gardner* left Blackwall for the arduous voyage to Madras and onto China. Following normal practice she called at Gravesend for passengers and a pilot. He guided her through the sandbanks of the Thames Estuary, around the North Foreland to anchor in the Downs. Here, with the Indiaman *Britannia*, she waited for a fair wind. Instead a gale blew up and they were driven onto the Goodwin Sands.

In the late 1970s and early 1980s four Indiamen were found: *Admiral Gardner, Britannia* and two which called at Gravesend but failed to clear the Thames. Dredgers winning sand for construction of Dover Hoverport were responsible for one Goodwins discovery, divers for the second, while commercial salvors using bucket grabs located the Estuary wrecks. The identity of *Albion* lost in 1765 and *Hindostan* in 1803 was only discovered when salvors allowed a few archaeologists to record the material which had been deposited with the Receiver of Wreck.

Other East Indiamen, such as *Earl of Abergavenny* (1805) near Weymouth, and *Henry Addington* (1798) on the Isle of Wight, have also been found. However, they are not so well preserved as those in the Goodwins and the Thames.

The degree to which the shifting sands could preserve ships was made clear when Richard Larn described *Admiral Gardner* to the Diving Conference at Bovisand in 1984. A substantial part of one side of the hull was believed to be intact, and there were many anchors and guns. Approximately one million copper East India Company coins had been recovered. Some were still packed inside barrels. The coins were for trade between ports in the East. The many copper ingots, stamped by the Rose Copper Company of Redruth, had the same purpose. There was also door furniture, still packed, part of a consignment for Bengal.

Nautical archaeologists requested an emergency designation of *Admiral Gardner* to prevent uncontrolled salvage. The protection was short-lived as it was successfully challenged on the grounds that she was actually outside the 3-mile territorial limit. Its extension to 12 miles enabled her to be re-designated in 1989.

Display of copper coins from Admiral Gardner *at Porthleven Wreck & Rescue.*

Viewpoint: the site is about 5km (3 miles) offshore on the Goodwin Sands (see Chapter 7)
Display: Charlestown Shipwreck & Heritage Centre
Further reading: Larn. R & B. 1995. *Shipwreck Index of the British Isles*. Volume 2 (listing).

SOME SHIPWRECKS
OF THE EAST INDIA COMPANIES

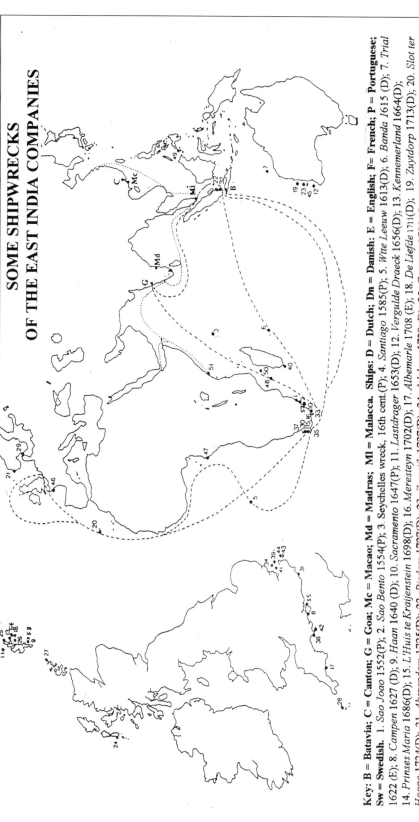

Key: B = Batavia; C = Canton; G = Goa; Mc = Macao; Md = Madras; Ml = Malacca. Ships: D = Dutch; Dn = Danish; E = English; F= French; P = Portuguese; Sw = Swedish. 1. *Sao Joao* 1552(P); 2. *Sao Bento* 1554(P); 3. Seychelles wreck, 16th cent.(P); 4. *Santiago* 1585(P); 5. *Witte Leeuw* 1613(D); 6. *Banda* 1615 (D); 7. *Trial* 1622 (E); 8. *Campen* 1627 (D); 9. *Haan* 1640 (D); 10. *Sacramento* 1647(P); 11. *Lastdrager* 1653(D); 12. *Vergulde Draeck* 1656(D); 13. *Kennemerland* 1664(D); 14. *Prinses Maria* 1686(D); 15. *L'Huis te Kraijenstein* 1698(D); 16. *Meresteyn* 1702(D); 17. *Albemarle* 1708 (E); 18. *De Liefde* 1711(D); 19. *Zuytdorp* 1713(D); 20. *Slot ter Hooge* 1724(D); 21. *Akerendam* 1725(D); 22. *Risdam* 1727(D); 23. *Zeewijk* 1727(D); 24. *Adelaar* 1728 (D); 25. *Curaçao* 1729 (P); 26. *Vendela* 1737(Dn); 27. *Svecia* 1740 (Sw); 28. *Hollandia* 1743(D); 29. *Goteburg* 1745(Sw); 30. *Reijgersdaal* 1747(D); 31. *Amsterdam* 1749(D); 32. *Geldermalsen* 1752(D); 33. *Doddington* 1755(E); 34. S. Edinburgh Channel wreck, 18th cent.(Sw?); 35. *Nieuw Rhoon* 1776(D); 36. *Valentine* 1779(E); 37. *Middelburg* 1781(D); 38. *Halsewell* 1786(E); 39. *Albion* 1765(E); 40. *Winterton* 1792(E); 41. *Hindostan* 1803(E); 42. *Earl of Abergavenny* 1805(E); 43. *Admiral Gardner* 1809(E); 44. *Britannia* 1809(E); 45. *Batavia* 1629(D); 46. *Prince de Conty* 1746(F); 47. *Mauritius* 1609(D); 48. *Sussex* 1738(E); 49. *Griffin* 1761(E); 50 *Bredenhof* 1753(De); 51. *Santo Antonio de Tanna* 1829(P); 52. Poompuhar wreck, 18th cent.(Dn?); 53. *Concordia* 1786(Dn); 54. *Stockholm* 1745(Sw); 55. *Henry Addington* 1798(E). Based on a map by Mark Redknap, with additions.

7 Pirate Surprise

Hollywood has immortalised the buccaneers and pirates of the Americas. For European citizens of seventeenth and eighteenth-century coastal towns piracy was far from our popular celluloid images. It was a realistic, ever-present and fearful danger. The most feared pirates came from North Africa operating out of ports such as Tangier, and Sallee in Morocco. Their ships plagued the seas from North Europe to Newfoundland and, as well as capturing ships, they made coastal raids taking captives for ransom and slavery.

Piracy brought revenue to North Africa. At Sallee 10% of prizes were taken by the town's ruling body; and the Dey of Algiers extracted payments of tribute from European powers for short-lived promises to safeguard their ships from the depredations of his subjects. Dutch and English merchants were willing to trade guns, skins and textiles for gold, saltpetre and sugar. During their own squabbles North European countries were only too happy to see their opponents' ships taken by pirates.

With such double standards Europe was never able to rid itself of the 'barbary' or 'corsair' menace. Individual countries mounted diplomatic missions and, when the economic burden and insult was too great, punitive attacks. Their efforts were never concerted and the pirate powers were not subdued until an American fleet was sent to the Mediterranean in the nineteenth century.

The capture, use and sale of ships by pirates adds a further spice to the great melting pot of international exchange which is represented in the shipwrecks around the British coast.

Schiedam
The Lizard, Cornwall

General Location: SW 6564 2062
Protection: 50° 02.33'N 05° 16.4'W, 75m radius
           HISTORICAL
Built: Holland
Type: fluit
Dimensions: between 20 and 40m
Lost: 4 April 1684
Voyage: Tangier to England
Cargo: army siege stores
Complement: 120 crew

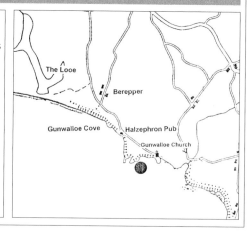

The history of *Schiedam* shows the pirate surprise which can confront the wreck detective. Her original name was *Great Schiedam* after the medieval town on the River Meuse. She was a Dutch fluit, a roomy and seakindly yet fast cargo carrier. It was the efficiency of these vessels which ensured that Dutch merchant ships carried the bulk of Europe's trade. Their size varied between 66 and 133ft (20-40m) in length and 200-400 tons. They had a vertical stem, bluff bows and were nearly flat floored. Typical cargoes included timber, wine and corn.

In 1683 *Schiedam* collected a cargo of timber from Ribadus in Northern Spain but on 1 August she was captured off Gilbralter by a 14-gun pirate ship. Her captivity was short-lived as the pirates were chased by Admiral Clowdisley Shovell in the 'gally frigate' *James*. Having captured *Schiedam* he took her into Cadiz where the timber was sold. From here she sailed with the English fleet under Lord Dartmouth on a punitive expedition against the pirate's stronghold, serving as a water-carrier.

The plan was to evacuate English merchants from Tangier, and to destroy the harbour mole and city defences. After the action *Schiedam* was loaded with army miners, ordnance, horses and English property and sent back to England. She reached the Channel but was wrecked in a gale at Gunwalloe on 4 April 1684. Her master had, reportedly, mistaken the coast for part of France.

The wreck was discovered in July 1971 by Anthony Randall. It lies close to Halzephron Headland and can be overlooked from the cliff path. After wrecking the ship was salvaged but how would its Dutch ownership, Spanish trading, pirate then English capture, and participation at Tangier feature in the seabed remains three centuries later?

When the site was found there were 16 iron cannon and some ship structure, including the rudder which was recovered. Their good preservation was explained when a shift in the seabed covered the site with 3-3.6m (10-12ft) of sand for nearly seven years. Such changes occur periodically, though unpredicatably, around the Lizard.

The ship was identified as *Schiedam* principally by the date of objects which matched documentary evidence. The key date is 1675 marked on a lead container. The container, one of three from the site, is a mystery as its function is unknown.

Viewpoint: the South West Coast Path passes Halzephron Headland, off which Schiedam *lies.*

While Anthony Randall holds most recovered objects some are displayed at Charlestown Shipwreck & Heritage Centre. Their precise origins and use are hard to prove but they have been linked to the story of the ship. For example, copper cooking kettles and the copper hoops, which once bound the staves of powder barrels, are described as the military equipment of the returning army. Undiagnostic pieces of marble and brass castings are also tentatively attributed to the assault on Tangier and the returning military ordnance.

Only the most robust of *Schiedam*'s contents have survived, so they are a very limited selection of all the objects, large and small, which could have been found aboard. It shows that even when a ship's history is known it is not always easy to relate precisely the wreck material to its building, ownership and voyages. It may be impossible to decide the identity of a ship for which there is no written information.

Mystery lead containers link this wreck site with the Royal Navy as the only others found have come from English warships dated 1690-1750.

Display: Charlestown Shipwreck & Heritage Centre
Further reading: Larn R. & B. 1995. *Shipwreck Index of the British Isles.* Volume I (listing)

Salcombe Cannon
Salcombe Bay, Devon

General Location: SX 752 367
Protection: 50° 12.696'N 03° 44.679'W, 250m radius
ARCHAEOLOGICAL
Lost: probably mid-seventeenth century

Gold coins and jewellery fuelled media coverage of this, the most recently designated Historic Wreck. Unusually, press and television reporters gathered at the British Museum to hear its discovery announced in November 1997. Once again divers had made finds which outstripped information from land sites and set challenges for museums, historians and collectors of art.

Salcombe Cannon Site is actually an old name and diving haunt. It lies in 18 - 20m of water off Deckler's Cliffs. For at least fifteen years divers from South-West Maritime Archaeological Group had known of the guns. They had found no other wreck material and it did not rate particular interest from the group who also found the Erme Estuary and Erme Ingot sites. Everything changed when, in April 1995, Ron Howell spotted a small piece of gold wedged in a fissure.

Over the next two years the team searched the deep rock gullies of the area. They recovered: more than 400 gold coins; tiny gold ingots made by pressing a finger into moist clay to make a mould; and gold earrings and pendants. All the gold has come from Morocco. British Museum staff are excited on two counts. Firstly, the seabed haul is the largest assemblage of Islamic coins ever found in the UK. Secondly, jewellery of the same design is still made and worn today and this is the first time that archaeology has provided precise dates for its earlier use.

The coins provide a date for the jewellery and the shipwreck. The coins were minted by the Moroccan dynasty called the Sa'did sharifs. Over a hundred were struck for Ahmad al-Mansur (ruled 1578-1603) and a further hundred for his son Mawlay Zaydan (ruled 1608-27). However the ship can only have been wrecked after the latest coins were minted. They were struck for al-Walid between 1631 and 1636.

There is, of course, a financial value to the gold. The team had followed the correct

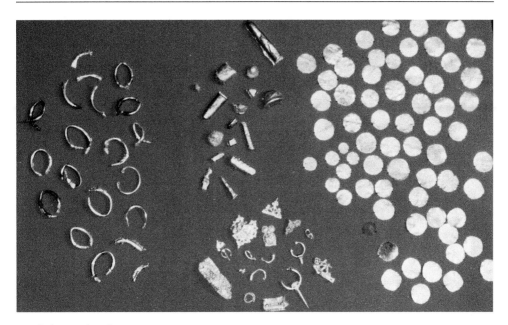

Finds from Salcombe cannon site.

procedure by reporting their finds to the Receiver of Wreck. For any recovered material it is the Receiver's responsibility to seek an owner and arrange for salvors to be reimbursed or, in the absence of an owner, to have material valued and sold. In this case the net proceeds are expected go to the diving team who have expended their own resources in its recovery. The British Museum are keen to purchase the collection if they have sufficient funds. Now that the site is designated any further work will be subject to the licensing conditions.

So far no documented wreck has been found to match the seabed discovery. Apart from the gold, with its African origin, there are other artefacts to consider. These include two copper coins only one of which is sufficiently well-preserved for identification. It was struck in Friesland in 1627. This, with some Delft pottery, gives a Dutch link. It seems the nationalities of objects from this mystery ship, by coincidence, mirror the history of the *Schiedam*. Further research into individual objects may find more tracks to follow. There are, for example, a fish-shaped lead sounding weight, pharmaceutical jars complete with their contents, merchants' seals, pottery and pewter ware. The pewter and pottery also suggest that the ship sailed sometime around 1640.

There are many questions for the future including the need to determine if the original guns and the new finds come from the same ship. Inside concretions are locked other treasures to bring the past alive, for example broad beans, complete and undecayed. They were probably roasted and eaten, like peanuts, as a delicacy.

Viewpoint: from the South West Coast Path the site is overlooked from Gara Rock Hotel on Bolt Tail

Collections: purchase has yet to be agreed (January 1998)

Wrangels Palais
Out Skerries, Shetland

General Location: HU 704 719

Protection: 60° 25.50'N 00° 43.27'W, 100m radius

HISTORICAL

Built: 1662, Holland

Type: Swedish warship captured by Danes

Dimensions: 33.6m x 8m (110ftx26 English ft)

Armament: 38 guns

Lost: 23 July 1687

Voyage: anti-pirate patrol off North Sea

Complement: 240

Saved: 152

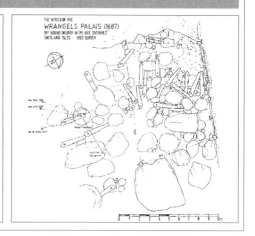

THE WRECK OF THE WRANGELS PALAIS (1687) OFF BOUND SKERRY IN THE OUT SKERRIES' SHETLAND ISLES · 1993 SURVEY

The British mainland is strategically positioned to control the English Channel. During hostilities North European countries sometimes sent ships north round Scotland to avoid English naval vessels and privateers. In 1664 the East Indiaman *Kennemerland* was wrecked on Shetland while on this 'achter om' route. Such a richly-laden vessel would have made a fine prize and, while East Indiamen might defend themselves, less well-armed ships could be taken.

For Denmark, pirates in these far northern waters could threaten not only merchant ships but her subjects in the Faroes and Iceland. The threat in 1687, said to be 13 Turkish vessels, was to be countered by a small naval force patrolling the open sea. On 23 July they encountered thick fog and *Wrangels Palais* struck rocks off Lamda Stack in the Out Skerries, Shetland.

Little is known of the circumstances surrounding the accident. It was first recorded in the log of the accompanying *Heyren* but *Wrangel Palais'* own log has not been traced. The captain and 87 seamen drowned but 152 survived including Lieutenant Joergan Liebedantz who was blamed for losing the ship.

Wrangels Palais began life under Swedish colours. She was named after a castle in Old Stockholm built by Marshal Carl Gustav Wrangel, who was a brave and accomplished Swedish officer who made his fortune from the spoils of war. He probably funded the building of *Wrangels Palais* or purchased her ordnance. *Wrangels Palais* was built in Holland in 1662 and put into the Swedish Navy in 1669. A nineteenth-century Swedish publication gives her dimensions in Swedish feet, (equivalent to 297mm). However, according to research by Lisberg Jensen, Director of the Royal Danish Naval Museum, the more reliable guide is two distinct but concurring Danish records. These use the Danish foot which is equivalent to 313.8mm. Converted into modern units they show that *Wrangels Palais* was 33.57m long, 8m broad and 3.6m deep with 38 guns.

Sweden and Denmark were old adversaries and in 1675 open conflict returned. It was during this Scanian War that *Wrangels Palais* was taken by the Danes. She was captured in 1677 when the Danish fleet, commanded by Niels Juel, broke through the Swedish blockade of their sea routes. *Wrangels Palais* was taken into Juel's Baltic fleet. Her name was left unchanged as a continuing irritant to her former owners. Her career prior to the anti-pirate patrol is little documented.

The wreck was discovered in August 1990. Dr Tim Sharpe, a member of Strathclyde University SAC, found some 20 cannon in a 24m deep rock gully off Bound Skerry. Two bronze cannon were raised. The clue to the site's identity as *Wrangels Palais* came from the date of 1677 inscribed on one of the guns. Salvage was halted by designation. A survey licence was issued in 1991 and in subsequent seasons members of the club took advantage of the NAS Training (Part I) which had recently won grant-aid from the Department of National Heritage.

By 1994, a total of 30 guns had been found and mapped on the *Wrangels Palais* site. The absence of other objects was put down to the ship actually striking some 750m away on Lamda Stack. The nearby *Kennemerland* site has shown that the actual wrecking process can be modelled through intensive analysis of a seabed survey.

Taking place at the same time was the first large-scale study of a substantial Scandinavian vessel since the *Wasa* and *Kronan* excavations. *Nelde Bladet* (1672) was a Danish warship comparable in size to *Wrangels Palais*. She was wrecked off Nice in 1693 after passing into the merchant service. However, she still retained equipment from her naval days which could provide comparative material for *Wrangels Palais* in the future.

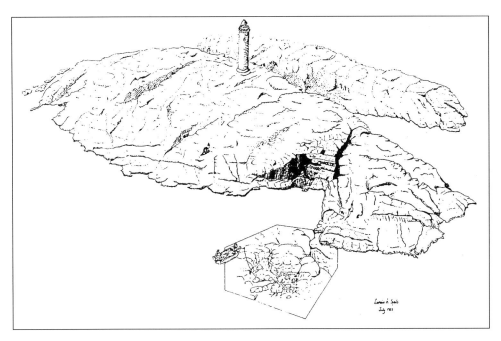

This artist's impression shows the relationship of the wreck site to Bound Skerry. The cannon lie in a rocky basin, backed by the rocks of the Skerry and fronted by a cliff dropping into deep water.

Viewpoint: this remote site is not easily visited, though there is a ferry to the Out Skerries
Further reading: Bound, M. & Sharpe, T. 1995. The wreck of the Danish man-of-war *Wrangels Palais* (1687) off Bound Skerries (Shetland Isles). In, Bound, M. (ed.). *The Archaeology of Ships of War*, Volume I: 45-7

Royal Anne
The Lizard, Cornwall

General Location: SW 6939 1140

Protection: 49° 57' 27"N 05° 12 56"W, 100m radius

HISTORICAL

Built: 1709, Woolwich Dockyard. Stacey

Type: 5th Rate 'gally'

Dimensions: 127 x 31ft (38.7 x 9.5m)

Armament: 42 guns

Lost: 10 November 1721

Voyage: Plymouth to Barbados

Complement: 247 crew

Saved: 3 people

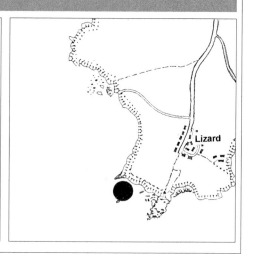

Sugar is a commodity which we take for granted. Elizabeth I's bad teeth were attributed to her girlhood passion for 'comfits' as sweets were called. It was in her reign that the Barbary Company was set up to improve trade with Morocco. This meant English ships could reach North Africa, unmolested by corsairs, to bring back sugar, dates and almonds to satisfy the English sweet tooth.

England's success in trading with North Africa irked her European rivals. For Spain, her expansion into the Caribbean was worse. It began with islands in which Spain had shown little interest. Bermuda was occupied in 1612, St Kitts in 1624 and Barbados, Nevis, Antigua and Barbuda soon after.

The first colonists landed on Barbados in 1627. A thriving colony developed with 2000 people, including white indentured labourers. They grew fruits and vegetables, for local consumption, and cotton and tobacco for export. In the 1640s the first sugar cane plants were tried and thrived in the climate. The new crop offered huge profits and changed the islands.

Slaves were imported from Africa to supply the labour needed on the plantations and soon outnumbered the Europeans by more than six to one. Sugar rapidly replaced tobacco for which the climate of Virginia was more suitable. It became the only product of importance for the islands and of the highest importance to the home economy. From the mid-seventeenth century only English or colonial-built ships were allowed to bring home cargoes from the colonies which could then be re-exported. The Dutch who were the chief traders in the Caribbean in the early seventeenth century were the first to be affected, and soon were at war with England.

The economic importance of the islands to Europe made them a theatre of war in many conflicts throughout the eighteenth century. Raids were carried out to devastate plantations, destroy crops and capture slaves. The danger and misery was increased by the operations of pirates and buccaneers. The sugar ships increased to 300 tons or more to withstand the attacks of naval and pirate ships.

Today, visitors to Barbados can see the massed iron guns of the Garrison above

Bridgetown, pointing seawards. Below, St James' Church and Codrington College, home of a previous governor, show the very English culture which awaited Lord Belhaven when he left Portsmouth aboard *Royal Anne*. Avoiding the scandal of having murdered his wife he was to take up the Governorship of Barbados and along with his household was taking out the family silver.

There were only six galleys classified as such in the Royal Navy. They were an attempt to combine the advantages of sail and oar propulsion. The *Royal Anne Galley* was described at her launch, in June 1709, as 'a new invention under the direction of the Marquis of Carmarthen...being the finest that ever was built'.

She was a 5th rate with an armament of 42 guns and a crew of 247 who manned her 60 oars when need arose and provided a fighting force if boarded. Rowing could enable a galley to capture becalmed or slower ships. The notorious pirate, Captain Kidd, used *Adventure* galley which had been built for the Royal Navy in 1695. Another galley taken and used by pirates, *Whydah*, has been excavated off Cape Cod, Massachussetts, where she was wrecked in a violent storm in 1717.

Royal Anne was also caught in a storm. On 10 November 1721 a south-west gale drove her on to Stagg Rock on the Lizard. There were only three survivors. Subsequently 'a newly invented diving engine' was used to 'fish upon the wreck'.

In 1969 members of Bristol University SAC believed they had found the site. Their finds included 8 iron guns and silver coins dated 1710 to 1720. It was only in 1992 when Rob Serrat was diving nearby that a conclusive link with the *Royal Anne* was found. This was the Belhaven crest on a piece of cutlery. The designated wreck site is centred on this new area of finds.

A series of rock gullies are filled with large rocks overlying coarse sand and small stones. The rocks are removed with air-filled lifting bags during hand excavation of the gullies. Solid rock is found 15-40cm (6-16in) below but even in these shallow deposits layers can be discerned. However, the discovery of a diver's fin buckle and other modern material in the bottom layer shows that the sea or burrowing creatures mix the content of some gullies.

Viewpoint: ten minutes along the South West Coast Path from the Lizard's southernmost cafes. It can also be seen looking westwards from the cafes.

A spoon handle bearing the Belhaven family crest proved the wreck site to be Royal Anne.

Sanitation

On ships the disposal of human waste was perfunctory. From medieval times barrels – 'necessary tubs' – were a convenience for the crew, and their contents were available in case of fire. A wooden box and seat was found on the fourteenth-century Bremen cog, but officers commonly used chamber pots before proper toilets were built into stern galleries, such as can be seen on *Victory*. Ships with a projecting beak had gratings beside the bowsprit through which waves freely drained, and these provided a hygenic, but terribly exposed, location for the 'heads', as the crew's toilet space was called.

Pewter chamber pot from the first royal yacht, Mary.

Pissdale pipe from the bow area of 5th Rate, Dartmouth.

Anonymous contemporary drawing of the heads on an early seventeenth-century ship.

8 Getting into Line

Ship-of-the-Line is one of those romantic naval expressions which suggest a long tradition of British supremacy at sea. In fact the first ships designed specifically for the tactic of fighting in a line astern, each ship pouring repeated broadsides into the enemy, were ordered in 1677. The 'Thirty Ships' were an innovation. For the first time naval dockyards built ships to standard sizes, one 1st Rate, nine 2nd Rates and twenty 3rd Rates. No fewer than five of those thirty ships have been found and protected as Historic Wrecks.

Anne
Pett Level, East Sussex

General Location: TQ 8977 1362
Protection: 50° 53.42'N 00° 41.91'E, 75m radius
              HISTORICAL
Built: 1678, Chatham
Type: 3rd Rate
Dimensions: 151 x 40ft (46m x 12.2m)
Armament: 70 guns
Lost: 5 July 1689
Voyage: Battle of Beachy Head
Complement: 460

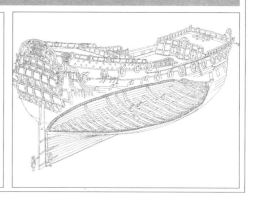

Launched in Chatham, *Anne* was among the six 3rd Rates completed by the naval dockyards in 1678. They were larger than any previous ship of their class except for two experimental vessels, *Edgar* (1668), whose remains are in the Solent, and *Royal Oak* (1674).

True to her design *Anne* stood in line at the Battle of Beachy Head on 30 June 1689. William & Mary had been chosen for the English throne and, with the Dutch as allies, England's adversary was now France. Queen Mary, who had been wrongly advised of the enemy's strength, ordered the outnumbered Anglo-Dutch fleet to engage. After seven hours of fighting the wind had died and the English Admiral, Torrington, decided to withdraw. *Anne* had lost her main and mizen masts. Despite a tow from *Swallow* and *York*, Captain Tyrrel had no hope of keeping up. He beached his ship and got his men and guns ashore before burning the hull to prevent the French taking her as a prize.

The bottom 2m (6ft 6in) of *Anne*'s hull is still embedded in the beach. Locals can remember playing among the timbers when they stood proud of the sand and the remains of three masts were visible. Today it can be seen on the lowest tides though sandbanks and pools sometimes obscure the timbers and the surrounding mud is treacherous.

Anne was protected in March 1974 by emergency designation after a mechanical excavator was used to pull objects out of the hull. Unfortunately not all of these can be traced but a few were handed to museums for conservation. They are small items,

Difficult Choices

How can the relative funding merits be decided between ships? There are not only many types of ship but different kinds of preservation. How can judgements be made between ships preserved: in archaeological sites such as *Anne*; in dock exhibits such as *Cutty Sark*; and maintained in operation like *Waverley*?

   The National Historic Ships Committee aims to advise funding agencies on museum and operational ships. It received a grant from the then Department of National Heritage to devise a system based on scores awarded against set criteria. These include many used to evaluate land sites: such as degree of rarity; representation of type; amount of documentation; and association with historical events. In contrast to using a mechanism aimed at objectivity, the Advisory Committee on Historic Wreck Sites takes decisions by weighing such factors informally.

including cast-iron grenades complete with wooden fuses, cannon balls and lead shot, and the staves from a barrel.

Although nearly two centuries had passed since her loss *Anne* was technically still a naval ship and belonged to the Ministry of Defence. In 1983 an important precedent was set for the care of historic naval wrecks. Ownership was transferred to the Warship Anne Trust which had been formed by the Trustees of the Hastings Shipwreck Heritage Centre. Their plans to move the hull to a purpose-built museum have been rekindled by the hopes of National Lottery funding. It would be a great tourist attraction for the seaside town to have the hull on show every day in its conservation tank. Plans to include a training pool to teach divers about survey would be beneficial for nautical archaeology. Volunteers are already getting involved. In September 1997 they helped to resurvey the hull.

Rate Specifications and Actual Dimensions of Ships in this Chapter

	1st	2nd	CO	3rd rate	AN	RE	ST	NO
Gundeck Length	165' 0"	158' 0"	160' 6"	150' 0"	150' 10"	150' 6"	152' 0"	152' 0"
Keel Length						124' 0"	126' 8"	126' 8"
Breadth	46' 0"	44' 0"	45' 0"	39' 8"	40' 0"	40' 0"	40' 6"	40' 4"
Depth in Hold	19' 2"	18' 4"	25' 11"	17' 2"	17' 0"	17' 0"	17' 8"	17' 3"

Origin of the Line

Elizabethan sea captains had all-round gun power. To attack they sailed towards an enemy ship firing their forward facing guns, fired a broadside, swung away firing their stern guns and turned around to use the other broadside. As reloading was difficult they hoped that this single manoeuvre would sufficiently disable the enemy for them to attempt a boarding. Sea battles were a free-for-all.

During the English Civil War small fast ships, frigates, were developed. Being relatively long and narrow most of their guns were on their broadsides. At the Battle of Gabbard (1653) the military thinking of Cromwell's generals was thrown against the Dutch. For the first time larger English ships, with guns concentrated on their broadsides, fought in a disciplined line-of-battle. Their victory practically won that First Dutch War.

In the Second Dutch War (1664-7) the English navy suffered an humiliating attack in Chatham, their home base. At the end of the Third (1672-4) the navy was left to decay. As England was increasingly allied with Holland, MPs were suspicious of the King's requests for new ships. It took Charles II helped by his Secretary of the Navy, Samuel Pepys, three years to persuade them. The money was finally voted in 1677 when they saw the growth of the French navy. By then Charles II and Pepys were committed to a new navy with larger vessels built to standard size. Their system of 1st, 2nd and 3rd Rate ships capable of fighting in line-of-battle was the foundation of naval practice throughout the eighteenth century.

Viewpoint: East of Pett from the seawall opposite where the Royal Military Canal swings inland
Display: Shipwreck Heritage Centre, Hastings
Further reading: Marsden, P. & Lyon, D. 1977. A wreck believed to be the warship *Anne*, lost in 1690. *International Journal of Nautical Archaeology*, 6.1: 9-20

Stirling Castle (see Colour Plate 13)
Goodwin Sands, Kent

General Location: TR 4468 5864
Protection: 51° 16.426′N 01° 30.516′E, 50m radius
      HISTORICAL
Built: 1679, Deptford Dockyard, John Shish
Type: 3rd Rate
Dimensions: 152 x 40ft (46.3 x 12.3m)
Armament: 70 guns
Rebuilt: 1699, Chatham   **Lost:** 27 November 1703
Voyage: anchored Downs   **Complement:** 349 crew   **Saved:** 70

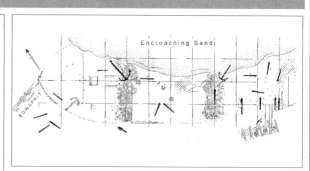

Memories of the devastation wreaked by the 1987 hurricane are still vivid. Similar memories were left by the Great Storm of 1703. The author of *Robinson Crusoe*, Daniel Defoe, wrote a book recording the destruction and death all round the British Isles. At the time England and France were at war. In the storm the English navy lost a dozen ships and about 2000 men. Four of these, which were in a squadron patrolling the Channel, had anchored in the Downs. The south-westerly wind drove them onto the notorious Goodwin Sands. The 3rd Rates, *Stirling Castle*, *Northumberland* and *Restoration,* were lost; all had been built a quarter of a century earlier as part of the Thirty Ships programme. An old 4th Rate, *Mary* (1650), was lost with them.

In 1979 a local archaeological society, the Thanet Archaeological Unit, was approached by five local divers: John Cayzer, John Chamberlain, Paul Fletcher, Roy Kennet and Keith Young. With the help of a Ramsgate fisherman, Tommy Brown, they wished to survey the Goodwin Sands. In July they began the huge task by diving to inspect places where the fisherman had snagged his nets or noted obstructions.

Late in the 1979 diving season they made an awe-inspiring discovery, a wooden warship more complete than *Mary Rose*. Other divers count themselves lucky to find a group of cannon, or a scatter of artefacts, or perhaps the ends of timbers from a buried hull fragment protruding through the seabed. All can be counted as important remains of shipwrecks. The Thanet team found themselves in another world, looking at a hull sitting on, not under, the seabed with guns in position, stores in the hold, and a huge copper kettle lying on deck amidst the remains of the galley hearth.

The size of the hull, the date of its contents and the mark of the naval broad arrow left no doubt that this was one of the 3rd Rates lost in the Great Storm. It was some time before detective work matched initials stamped on pewter plates with the officers of *Stirling Castle*.

Perhaps it is possible to have too much of a good thing. The ship's remains stood over 6m (20ft) high. While much of the bow and the transom superstructure had fallen away the main part of the hull was intact to the lower gun deck, with the hold being viewed through hatches in the deck. In places it survived to the gun ports and some guns were in place on their carriages. It seemed that the entire wreck had recently emerged from the deep sand.

The Downs and The Goodwin Sands

Before the great artificial harbours of Ramsgate and Dover were built a fleet could find little shelter between the Thames and the Solent. The Downs is an anchorage used by ships waiting for fair winds and tides either to make the tricky passage through the sand banks of the Thames Estuary or to run westward down the Channel. It is roughly 12 miles (20km) long and 3 miles (5km) wide, and lies inshore between St Margaret's Bay and Ramsgate. The anchorage offered little safety and Richard Larn has recorded 532 losses in the Downs. The boatmen of Deal are famed for their work there: ferrying supplies to ships, making heroic rescues and recovering wreck.

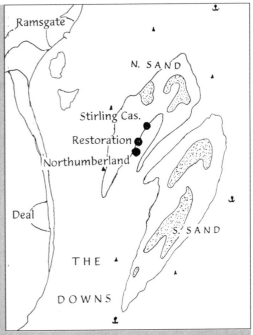

The Goodwin Sands lie eastward of the Downs. Comprising the North and South Sands they stretch for 7 miles (11km) and are 4 miles (6km) wide. The nearest point to land is just 2½ miles (4km) from Deal Pier. At low water parts of the sands dry out but once covered they become semi-mobile and anything heavy, such as a ship, sinks bodily into them. Hence the seamen's name 'ship-swallower'.

Indeed, lying with its bows to the west, its starboard side was still engulfed in a massive sandbank. The sand had preserved virtually everything except iron and human flesh. With enough stores and equipment for 349 men to sail and fight the ship it was truly like finding a small castle abandoned by defenders who had no time to collect their military, domestic or personal possessions.

For such a discovery on land there would undoubtedly be a high-profile, funded, emergency response aiming to evaluate the threats and take appropriate action. Ideally a painstaking process of recording and research would precede display of the whole wonderful find to the public.

Taking advice the local team adopted the best available strategy for rapid survey. The ship was 'roped' to divide the hull along its centreline and into 15ft (4.5m) lengths from stern to bow. Each area could be surveyed, drawn, photographed and excavated. With plans to investigate fully in 1980, efforts focused on exploring and lifting any objects which seemed at immediate risk from the sea or 'treasure seekers'.

Sadly, when the first dive was made in 1980 the spectacular hull had vanished.

View point: Deal seafront
Displays: Ramsgate Maritime Museum
Further reading: Perkins, D. nd. *The Great Storm Wrecks*; Cates, M & Chamberlain D. 1998. In Bound, M (ed.). *The Archaeology of Ships of War. Volume 2*

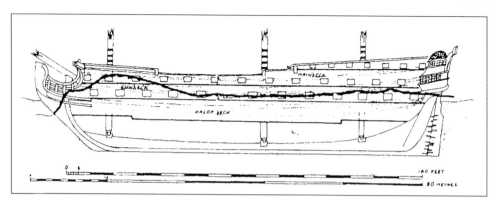

A line drawn on the side of a typical 3rd Rate hull shows the level to which Stirling Castle *survived.*

Dave Perkins' impression of the hull when it was exposed in 1979.

Northumberland
Goodwin Sands, Kent

General Location: TR 4432 5681	**Armament**: 70 guns
Protection: 51° 15.45'N 01° 30.12'E, 50m radius	**Rebuillt**: 1702/3 Chatham
HISTORICAL	**Lost**: 26 November 1703
Built: 1679, Bristol. Bayley	**Voyage**: anchored Downs
Type: 3rd Rate	**Complement**: 253 crew
Dimensions: 152 x 40ft (46.3 x 12.3m)	**Saved**: None

Once Parliament agreed the Thirty Ships programme, facilities had to be found to construct many vessels at once. Pepys had hoped to build them all in naval yards where a close eye could be kept on quality. However capacity was soon taken up with the large 1st and 2nd Rates. *Northumberland* was the first 3rd Rate to be built under contract. Her hull was laid down in Bristol by Francis Bayley. Delays caused by timber shortages meant she was not launched until 1679. By this time Pepys had already realised that the naval dockyards lacked the capacity to complete all 30 ships in a short time and more were placed to contract.

By 1684 the vessels built under the programme were showing signs of decay. Pepys had to defend his choice of non-naval yards and his investigation into the problem finally laid the blame on poor maintenance once the ships were in commission. Repairs were put in hand to bring the ships up to scratch.

Close study of well-preserved hulls can reveal repairs and alterations made during a vessel's life. For the three vessels lost on the Goodwins this would theoretically be a complex process. A dozen or so years after the repairs made by Pepys they were all taken in for such substantial work that they were considered 'rebuilt'. *Northumberland* was still in the yards when *Stirling Castle* was recommissioned in 1701.

Northumberland was found in 1980, a small compensation for the disappointment caused by the movement of sands obliterating *Stirling Castle*. In contrast to the completeness of *Stirling Castle* the wreck site comprised mounds of debris. These did include some coherent pieces of ship's side with ribs, planking and lead scuppers in place. A ship's bell had played a part in the initial dating of *Stirling Castle,* and a similar bell was found on this site. Both were complete with their wooden stocks and were marked with the naval broad arrow and the date 1701. Again it was initials on pewter which suggested the identity of the wreck as *Northumberland*.

Viewpoint, Display and **Further reading**: see *Stirling Castle*

Bronze drake from Stirling Castle. The inscription tells that it was made by Assuerus Koster of Amsterdam in 1642. It fired a six pound shot and its own weight is marked in Dutch pounds as 682A. The broad arrow, the mark of the British Board of Ordnance, signifies its later acquistion by the Royal Navy. This shows the difficulty of using uninscribed guns to identify shipwrecks.

Navigational instruments in a sea chest included sand glasses, ranging from half minute for speed-reckoning to half hour for watch-keeping.

II (JJ) stamped on pewter plates found in the galley helped to identify Stirling Castle as they were the initials of her captain, John Johnson.

Restoration
Goodwin Sands

General Location: TR 4431 5709	**Armament:** 70 guns
Protection: 51° 15.60'N 01° 30.13'E, 50m radius	**Rebuilt:** 1701 Chatham
HISTORICAL	**Lost:** 26 November 1703
Built: 1678, Harwich. Betts	**Voyage:** anchored Downs
Type: 3rd Rate	**Complement:** 391 crew
Dimensions: 150 x 40ft (45.9 x 12.2m)	**Saved:** None

When *Northumberland* was found in 1980 a second site was also discovered. This likewise comprised mounds of debris from which divers recovered a huge copper kettle similar to the two found in the galley of *Stirling Castle* and recovered. The site has been protected as the remains of *Restoration*, although at the time its identity posed some questions. It might have been part of *Northumberland* or even the 4th Rate *Mary* which is known to have been lost with the other three ships.

Copper kettle from Northumberland *on display in Ramsgate Maritime Museum. It was positioned on the upper deck in a brick-built furnace which reduced the risk of fire spreading. On earlier wrecks, such as Cattewater, remains of open hearths and food debris are found in the hold.*

Viewpoint, Display and **Further reading**: see *Stirling Castle*.

Coronation (see Colour Plate 12)
Penlee Point, Cornwall

Inshore General Location: SX 4390 4860
Protection: 50° 18.96'N 04° 11.57'W 150m radius
Offshore General Location: SX 4339 4789
Protection: 50° 18.57'N 04° 11.98'W, 150m radius

HISTORICAL
Built: 1685, Portsmouth Naval Dockyard
Type: 2nd Rate
Dimensions: 160 x 45ft (48.9 x 13.7m)
Armament: 90 guns
Lost: 3 September 1691
Voyage: Channel blockade

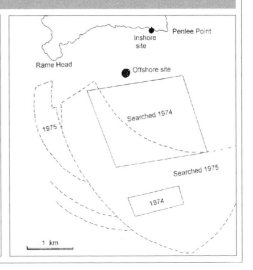

When *Coronation* finally slid from the shipways at Portsmouth Royal Dockyard in 1685 the Thirty Ships programme was complete. Back in 1677 Pepys' specification for the nine 2nd Rates had set 158ft (48.2m) for the gundeck enabling the ships to carry an awesome 90 guns on three decks. The number of guns for each rate was set by 'establishments' which were issued periodically. The number of guns aboard *Coronation* was to be a point of contention among divers who believed they had found her wreck site.

Coronation, captained by Skelton, had stood in the line with *Anne* at the Battle of Beachy Head. She survived only to meet her end two years later in a gale which was nearly as disastrous for the English Navy as the Goodwins losses in the Great Storm of 1703.

After the defeat at Beachy Head, Admiral Russell was given command of the Channel fleet. Wishing to bring the French to battle he tirelessly patrolled their coast. In some weathers it was impossible to hold station in the Channel and the fleet would turn for shelter in Torbay. In late August they set sail from Torbay only to be met by strong winds which on 2 September made them turn back for Plymouth.

The wind rose to a full gale. It blew from the south-south-west making the entrance to Plymouth Sound a hazardous course for the most experienced naval officer. The captains of *Harwich*, *Northumberland* and *Royal Oak* took on the challenge. They did not fare well, hitting rocks on Maker Point, grounding in the Hamoaze and going ashore under Mount Edgcumbe House. Other captains chose to anchor between Rame Head and Penlee and attempt to ride out the storm. Their logs record that *Coronation* was among them but they do not agree on the exact events of her loss. She sank with huge loss of life.

It is now more than thirty years since divers found first cannon balls and then cast-iron guns in the steep, gravel-filled rock gullies around Lady Cove. The Protection of Wrecks Act (1973) was still six years away. Convinced that they had found *Coronation* the divers took the steps which were then available to safeguard a wreck site, historic or otherwise, from interference. The seabed was leased from the Crown Estate Commissioners, a device used for *Mary Rose* before she could be designated. The Receiver of Wreck was

Viewpoint: the Victorian folly on Penlee Point overlooks the wreck sites with a view of Rame Head. On a grey and windy day it is a good place to imagine the events of 3 September 1691. The inshore site lies beside the rocky islet (bottom left).

informed, as were local authorities, and a small article was given to the local press. Today some teams still consider it more effective to warn off other divers by establishing their rights to a historic wreck through leases or salvage law than by turning to the Protection of Wrecks Act.

In the 1950s and 1960s underwater archaeology was in its infancy. Headlines were made by Roman and Greek wrecks in the Mediterranean. Here in Britain those eager to show that wrecks in home waters were as worthwhile formed the Council for Nautical Archaeology. For the sake of maritime history, archaeological recording needed to keep pace with the salvage of shipwrecks.

Alan Bax took up the cause and ran the first training courses in the School for Nautical Archaeology, Plymouth, now better known as Bovisand. In 1970 the diving magazine *Triton* carried a detailed report of SNAP's survey on the Penlee cannon site. It describes their pioneering search for successful measuring and tagging techniques in underwater survey. Today the measuring techniques are refined and computer programmes help to resolve the results into reliable site plans. The training is now available both in Britain and abroad through the Nautical Archaeology Society's Training Programme.

Despite careful survey the SNAP divers were unable to tally the number and measurements of the seabed guns with those reckoned to be aboard *Coronation*. It is a problem which has beset many sites, perhaps most notably Tearing Ledge. Their difficulties fuelled cynicism over the identity of the site. Richard Larn tackled the problem in *Devon Shipwrecks* (1974) saying that the site was too close to shore and too shallow to be *Coronation* which was reported lost in 22 fathoms (44m).

If this was not *Coronation* Peter McBride determined to find it. He began with documents, plotting the movements of the whole 28-ship squadron using 110 officers' logs preserved in the Public Record Office. His findings agreed with Larn: the wreck must lie roughly 1-3km offshore. Over five years seabed searches progressed from drift dives, to magnetometer survey first guided by a sextant operator, and finally following decca lanes.

By August 1977 the chosen search area had been completely scoured without success. The team opted to move inshore to depths of 20m. An anomaly was found which on inspection appeared to be a single cannon buried muzzle-first in the seabed. The full site was found 240m to the north-north-east, a scatter of cannon spread over a seabed of rocky mounds and sandy depressions. The identity was indisputable when Peter McBride found a folded pewter plate bearing the family crest of Captain Charles Skelton. His quest had taken 2813 man hours to cover nearly 12 million square metres of seabed with 4260 minutes of deep water diving.

Early work on the two sites produced a cannon tally of 53 inshore and 15 offshore. The search for an explanation of the two sites turned to wrecks such as *Kennemerland* for which eye-witness accounts told of the ship breaking up with one part sinking in deep water while the other drove ashore. The seabed finds of cannon, galley bricks and small artefacts bear out their story.

In recent years Peter McBride joined forces with Plymouth Maritime Archaeological Interest Group to resurvey the area. They are also seeking information from the many people who, over the years, have dived Penlee. Global positioning systems, remote sensing and computer plots are being used to integrate old and new observations. Meticulous mapping over a wide area will help finally to resolve the last moments of the *Coronation*.

Further reading: Larn, R & B. 1995. *Shipwreck Index of the British Isles*. Volume 1 (listing)

9 Fast Vessels

Twentieth-century life is fast. When a juggernaut can thunder past family cars on the motorway it is hard to discern the compromises in design between the competing needs for speed, carrying space and safety. Sailing ships all relied on the same power source. The wind was equal for all and it was their individual hull shape and rig which determined their speediness. Merchants with low value bulky goods like coal or grain and naval commanders eager to carry many large guns were willing to sacrifice fast sailing qualities for capacious, stable hulls. Longer, narrow hulls were given to ships where speed was important. For the navy small fast ships could keep pace with nimble pirate ships, scout out the enemy, and carry urgent messages. For the civilian they could be used for pleasure. For the government they could carry the mails.

Duart Point
Sound of Mull, Highlands

General Location: NM 7481 3546
Protection: 56° 27.45'N 05° 39.32'W, 75m radius

HISTORICAL

Built: 1640s
Type: early frigate-type
Lost: 13 September 1653
Voyage: punitive expedition to Mull

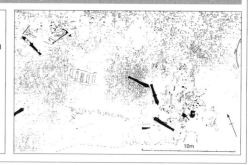

The thrill that comes when hours of research suddenly throw a clear light on a ship's past often has to be kept private in the silence of a library. Dr Colin Martin's delight over the Duart Point Wreck was obvious from his letter:

> By the way, we've also made something of a breakthrough in the historical research, identifying the ship as one of quite exceptional interest and importance. She was, it appears, a conscious attempt by Charles I to replicate a Dunkirk privateer as a counter to piracy in the Irish Sea, and so she ranks as one of the earliest frigate-types to be built in England. The archaeological potential is stunning.

Since it was reported in 1991 the site has ranked among the best models for managing a Historic Wreck.

The wreck was found by a visiting diver, John Dadd, who hoped to return to the site. Twelve years later, realising that he would never have time, he reported it in order to see the ship responsibly investigated. The Archaeological Diving Unit (ADU) inspected the site, which included structure and guns and was dated by seventeenth-century pottery, and recommended designation. Before designation was in place the Dumfries & Galloway Scottish SAC independently found the site and attempted to raise some guns. Once told of the situation they joined the work to safeguard and study the site.

When the ADU visited in the following year there were signs of erosion. The site was no longer stable. Historic Scotland funded rescue work in which the ADU recorded and then packaged 83 vulnerable objects. It was an unprecedented action as the agencies administering the Protection of Wrecks Act had never before funded rescue or research. Historic Scotland kept up their commitment by providing subsistence and travelling expenses for winter monitoring.

The Scottish Institute for Maritime Archaeology, members of the ADU and the Dumfries & Galloway Club made regular visits. They were therefore able to take action when erosion uncovered a deposit containing rope, a wooden block, a rammer head, a shoe, staves and wooden panelling. It was a challenge for any excavator or conservator. A decision was made. The deposit was carefully recorded, then covered with aggregate. In the short-term, at least, this has provided a barrier to further erosion.

Five weeks of survey in 1993 was completed by placing 240 loosely filled polyesterweave sandbags over the most vulnerable areas. After winter monitoring the 1994 season was used to produce a 1:10 scale drawing of 25 x 25m of seabed in just 116 underwater hours. The site has also been used for studies of corrosion and the deterioration of organic materials.

A minor breakthrough came in 1995 when the site was opened to the public for three days. It had taken twenty-two years for the Protection of Wrecks Act to be interpreted so that a licensee team could show small numbers of visiting divers around a site.

What has this exemplary site produced? Interim academic reports and colourful magazine articles present the unusually well-preserved group of mid-seventeenth-century objects. These explain the link with the small vessel, *Swan*. She had been sent by Cromwell from Ayr, in company with two others to combine with three ships sailing from Leith to close the Western Isles to Dutch landings. They had entered the Sound of Mull as a show of force against the traditionally Royalist clan MacLean. *Swan* and *Martha & Margrett* were driven ashore in a violent storm on 13 September 1653.

The identity of the *Swan* is clinched by wonderfully preserved wooden carvings. The ornate sterns of seventeenth-century English ships are known from paintings but are not expected to survive a shipwreck. Those from *Swan* are the only surviving carvings found in British waters. They include the ostrich feathers forming the badge of the heir apparent to the English throne; the national symbols of Scotland and Ireland; and a much publicised cherub. Dr Colin Martin suggests that when the Royalist ship was captured her crew took down the carvings but then stowed them in the hold. This would account for their survival in the bottom of the ship. At least 15m x 5m (49x16ft) of structure is held

Frigates

An effective navy must match the tactics of its adversary. In the 1620s small swift privateering vessels were attacking merchant ships in the Irish Sea and Western Approaches. In 1627 Charles I responded by building 10 identical ships called *1st, 2nd,...10th Lion Whelp*. Being scaled-down warships, they were relatively broad in proportion to their length, which combined with the weight of ten guns, meant they were not swift vessels.

Samuel Pepys also saw the need for small, fast, armed ships. *Constant Warwick* (1646) is said to have been modelled on the privateers built in Dunkirk. She is often called the first frigate. She carried 30 guns, had a 90ft (27.4m) keel and 28ft (8.5m) beam. *Adventure* was also built in 1646. Like the *Lion's Whelps* she had oar ports between her gun ports, a feature shared by several other early frigates. Frigates soon evolved to have two decks, more guns but no oars.

Soon any small fast armed vessel began to be called a frigate, and, by the end of the century, the name no longer applied to a specific naval vessel. However, the name 'Galley Frigate' was given to sail-oar hybrids. With 20 guns ranged along the upper deck, there were only two on the lower, leaving space amidships for oar ports.

The 'true frigates' were 5th and 6th Rate vessels developed from the 1740s. They had two decks, the upper being continuous (a 'tween deck). By carrying their guns on the upper deck they raised the height of the main battery but sat lower and were thus more sea-kindly. These early frigates had 28, 32 or 36 guns but by the end of the Napoleonic war they had grown in size and carried as many as 50 guns.

down beneath two areas of ballast between which it is visible. The discovery that *Swan* was a new departure in English shipbuilding makes all the more important study of her remains.

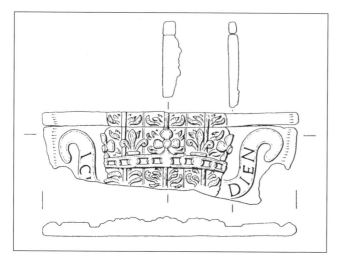

Badge of the heir apparent to the English throne (84cm/33in long). The surviving carving shows the lower parts of three ostrich feathers encircling a coronet with a scroll bearing the almost complete motto ICH DIEN.

A radiograph revealing the ornate wire-wound hilt of an English rapier inside an amorphous lump of concretion. Such images enable concretions to be carefully dissected in a laboratory with minimal damage to their contents.

Viewpoint: Duart Castle
Display: Duart Castle. Collections: National Museums of Scotland
Further reading: Martin, C. 1995. The Cromwellian shipwreck off Duart Point, Mull: an interim report. *International Journal of Nautical Archaeology*, 24.1: 15-32

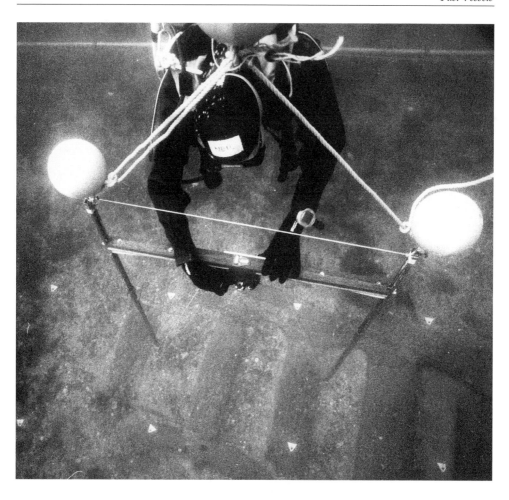

Good visibilty. A diving archaeologist from the Scottish Institute for Maritime Studies making a photomosaic of exposed structure on the Duart wreck.

Dartmouth
Sound of Mull, Strathclyde

General Location: NM 725 405
Protection: 56° 30.19'N 05° 41.95'W, 50m radius
       HISTORICAL
Built: 1655, Portsmouth Dockyard. John Tippets
Type: frigate
Dimensions: 80 x 25ft (24.4 x 7.6m)
Armament: 32 guns
Rebuilt: 1678

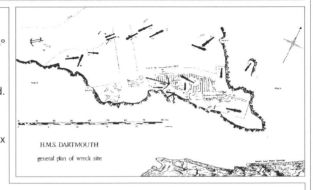

H.M.S. DARTMOUTH
general plan of wreck site

Lost: 9 October 1690 **Voyage:** punitive expedition to Mull **Complement:** approx 130 **Saved:** 6

Dartmouth is an example of an early frigate. She was built in 1655 and proved a good workhorse. Her long career ended during a punitive expedition against the Macleans similar to that undertaken by the *Swan* thirty seven years earlier. Oral tradition still recalls the 9 October 1690. A storm drove *Dartmouth* from anchor in Scallastle Bay stern-first across the Sound to ground on a small rocky islet, Eilean Rudha an Ridire.

The islet is a multiple shipwreck location. In 1973 Bristol University SAC were diving *Ballista* lost earlier that year and a 1930s vessel. To the north Jon Adnams discovered iron guns and a ship's bell. The holidaying team spent the remainder of two weeks locating guns and surveying the site. This included three days separating the bell from a gun, a process recorded on cine film. Marked 'DH 1678' it showed that they had found *Dartmouth*.

They reported the discovery to the Receiver of Wreck and sought advice from the Council for Nautical Archaeology. Dr Colin Martin agreed to assess the site which he visited in November. Unfortunately by the time designation came through in April 1974 unknown divers had caused damage by raising one anchor and attempting to raise a second. The finders formed the Bristol Undersea Archaeology Group and worked with the Scottish Institute for Maritime Studies. By 1978 they had spent twenty-four weeks on the site and believed they had identified its full extent.

Unlike the *Mary Rose*, *Amsterdam* and Goodwins wrecks which sank deep into preserving sand *Dartmouth* dug her own shallow grave. The whole site tells the story and bears out the local tale.

Her wreckage lies at the foot of a sloping rock face with its shoreward end in a wedge-shaped gully. Here were found objects from the stern of the ship, navigational and surgical instruments, fine pewter and ceramic tableware. Moving away from the shore the gully opens out. At this point lay the main portion of structure buried by 60cm (2ft) of sand and flint chippings which had probably been taken aboard as ballast in Plymouth. Broken guns and shot, too large for *Dartmouth's* armament, are probably also ballast. Beyond this area are further fragments of planking and objects which may have come from the boatswain's store in the bows of the frigate. Everything lies on a line WSW – ENE. On a parallel axis there are more guns and lead fittings.

This careful plotting allows the wreck event to be reconstructed. The wind drives *Dartmouth* across the Sound until her stern bumps on the ground with her bows to WSW. She heels to starboard and everything which is not fixed slides down the sloping decks to lie among the guns. The force of the impact has broken her back somewhere about the mainmast. In the pounding waves the bow tumbles over on the rocky ledge spilling guns away from the main hull. The stern is left with its port side out of the water taking the full battering of the weather. In time, as the ship breaks apart, the remaining keel and false keel, rocked by the force of the sea, dig themselves into the clay. While this ensured their preservation, the build up of mobile pebbles and ballast preserved the other fragments of the structure.

Dartmouth was built to a specification of 80ft keel and 25ft beam by 10ft depth of hold (24.4m x 7.6m x 3m). A section of surviving hull was recovered including over one fifth of the keel. The chance to dismantle this piece of hull was a unique opportunity to discover the construction of an early frigate. Historical documents give little more than the main dimensions with the realisation of lines and details of construction left to individual surveyors and shipwrights.

Following excavation the designation was revoked. However, fears that the site was being damaged and that further finds were being made led to a new designation. In 1994 the Sound of Mull Archaeological Project invited members of the Nautical Archaeology Society to take part in resurveying *Dartmouth*. A fifteen-man team spent seventy five underwater-hours producing a new site plan for comparison with the 1970s work. There was new material and some finds were from outside the original area of investigation.

A rare opportunity to discover how an early frigate was built. National Museums of Scotland conservators dismantling the recovered portion of Dartmouth's *hull.*

Viewpoint: Eilean Rudha an Ridire lies off a remote stretch of the mainland coastline without roads
Collections: National Museum of Scotland
Further reading: Martin, C. 1978. The *Dartmouth*, a British frigate wrecked off Mull, 1690. 5 The ship. *International Journal of Nautical Archaeology*, 7.1: 29-58

Mary (see Colour Plate 10)
Skerries, Gwynedd

General Location: SH 2651 9479

Protection: 53° 25′ 16″N 04° 36′ 40″W, 100m radius

HISTORICAL

Built: 1660

Type: yacht

Dimensions: 52 x 19ft (15.8 x 5.8m)

Armament: probably 8 guns

Lost: 25 March 1675

Voyage: Dublin to Chester

Complement: 74   **Saved:** 39

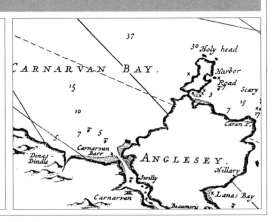

The 'first British yacht' was built by the Dutch East India Company (VOC). *Mary* was purchased by the City of Amsterdam, embellished and given to Charles II when he was restored to the English throne. The Dutch word 'yacht' derives from 'jagen' meaning to hurry or chase. Luxurious versions like *Mary*, with insignia and decoration on their counters, were used for tours of duty by officials. Yachts were built for speed and had leeboards in order to combine a large sail area with the shallow draught essential in Dutch waters. A long spar or sprit supporting the mainsail was soon changed to a shorter, less cumbersome gaff. They were excellent sailers and it was the jacht *Duyfken* which made the first recorded voyage to Australia. The Western Australian Maritime Museum is planning a full-size copy.

Contemporary information includes *Mary*'s dimensions and ordnance. Samuel Pepys sailed in her and noted: 'one of the finest things that I ever saw for neatness and room in so small a vessel. Mr Pett is to make one to outdo this for the honour of his country, which I fear he will scarce better.'

Lacking a deep keel, she was given more ballast for sailing in English waters. Charles enjoyed sailing against his brother and wanted a yet faster vessel. The following year *Katherine* was built for him by Phineas Pett, the first of some 26 yachts constructed for naval use in Charles' reign. *Mary* was demoted to general service, transporting officials between Dublin and Holyhead, the Irish Sea being described as 'so short and broken that Holland built ships are found fittest for that purpose'.

On 25 March 1675 she was en route from Dublin to Chester with a crew of 28, plus 3 noblemen and 43 other passengers. In thick fog while passing Anglesey in the small hours she struck the south-west corner of the Skerries near the site of the lighthouse built thirty-nine years later. Fortunately she caught in a gully with her long mast touching the rocks. About half those on board were able to scramble ashore where they spent a miserable couple of days before they were rescued.

The wreck quickly broke up and artefacts and guns lay on the bottom with concreted masses of iron shot. In July 1971 two diving groups, the Chorley and Merseyside SACs, independently, discovered a number of bronze cannon. Dr Peter Davies of Liverpool University mediated and a joint expedition with expert advisers was agreed. Meanwhile, however, looters removed at least four guns. As the 1973 Act had yet to be passed a rapid rescue operation recovered the remaining nine guns, finds and many lumps of concretion. These were taken to Liverpool City Museums Conservation Department to be stabilized.

Sporadic investigation of the site has now continued for over twenty-five years. Merseyside Museums have over 1,500 objects from the shipwreck. These include many items belonging to her noble passengers, such as silver cutlery and gold and diamond jewellery. Matthew Tanner is now reviewing all the old information and preparing a definitive report.

Contemporary illustration of the yacht Mary.

Viewpoint: the site cannot be seen from the mainland
Display: Merseyside Maritime Museum
Further reading: Davies, P. 1979. The discovery and excavation of the Royal Yacht Mary. *Maritime Wales*, 3: 25-73.

Hanover
St Agnes, Cornwall

General Location:
Protected Area: 50° 20.075'N 05° 10.823'W, 250m radius
HISTORICAL
Type: postal packet, brig
Lost: 6 December 1763
Voyage: Lisbon to Falmouth
Cargo: mails; specie
Complement: 67
Saved: 3

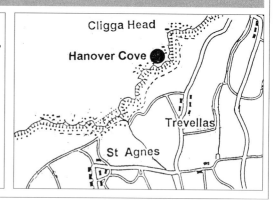

Naval ships, like *Mary*, were not the only vessels carrying important messages overseas. The Post Office set up services using fast ships which became known as packets. In 1689 they opened the Spanish packet service with three vessels ensuring a fortnightly run between Falmouth and Corunna. The first 270 miles (435km) of the journey from London were overland, but the large sheltered harbour at Falmouth was preferred to Plymouth because it was less exposed to French pirates. During the next century frequent conflicts with Spain forced a diversion to Lisbon, for which four vessels were required.

Packets needed to be swift and had to be armed for defence of their valuable mails. They had the right to take prizes, in other words, to capture any non-friendly vessels encountered on their route. In 1740 *Townshend* fell in with a 20-gun Spanish privateer and battled for seven hours before having to give in. The mails were thrown overboard before she hauled down her colours.

Few ships were lost on the route though the journey might take any time from the extremes of five to forty five days. On 6 December 1763 the Falmouth-bound packet brig *Hanover* was swept north of Land's End by a storm and driven onto the bare cliff face near St Agnes. Her cargo included gold specie. Insurers paid out for the total loss of one consignment but when in April 1765 'an iron trunk which contained all of Mr Michael Firth's bullion was fished up' the case made legal history. It established the principle that if an insurer paid out on lost cargo which was then restored to the owner without loss the insurer was entitled to be refunded.

The place in which she sank is called Hanover Cove. This is not the only instance of a ship's loss being recorded in a place-name and they are often used to locate wrecks.

Diver Magazine December 1996 reported that Colin Martin, a Cornish salvage diver, had gone public on his discovery of the wreck site. A bell and gold ring were his proof of its identity, both recovered when storms uncovered the ship in a sand-filled gully which he had dived many times before. To fund salvage, shares were issued offering a 1000% return through sale of cargo or as shares in a heritage centre. The Post Office, as owners, had paid for an archaeological assessment of the shipwreck but its recommendation and their application for the site to be designated was not granted. Designation was only made after a salvage rig was positioned on site and had raised more than fifty guns so destabilising the site. The salvor responded with litigation and was granted a licence to continue excavation under the watch of two archaeologists.

These events brought into question the operation of the Protection of Wrecks Act. It highlighted the need for mechanisms to integrate archaeological interests within legitimate marine activities including commercial salvage.

Viewpoint: Cligga Head, July 1997. The rig positioned on the site seen from the South West Coast Path. Between Blue Hills and Perranporth it passes over the cliffs above Hanover Cove. The cliff tops have many capped mine shafts and the cliff faces are stained green from old copper workings. Looking down into the cove it is easy to see why only three of Hanover's *40 passengers and 27 crew survived.*

Further reading: Larn, R & B. 1995. *Shipwreck Index of the British Isles.* Volume 1 (listing)

Ship's bell from the Hanover *packet clinched its identity*

Some of the iron guns being recovered from the site.

10 Timeless Traders

Merchant ships always outnumbered warships and their losses in peace and war far exceeded those of navies. Apart from those carrying valuable cargoes they rarely excite the sort of quest which brought the discovery of *Coronation* or *Mary Rose*. For merchant ships such searches would be more difficult as, in earlier centuries, their loss did not provoke the carefully recorded courts martial of naval shipwrecks. Yet the same lack of written information about the construction and operation of early merchant ships makes their wreck sites all the more important. Unfortunately, even when discovered, some merchant vessels remain anonymous, particularly if the cargo and other contents have been salvaged. While some cargoes, like fruit, perished quickly others such as stone pinned down and helped to preserve the hull which carried them. A cargo mound spotted by a diver or by remote sensing can be the first indication of a lost merchant ship.

Seaton Carew
Hartlepool, Teeside

General Location: NZ 2960 5298
Protection: 54° 39.50'N 01° 10.71'W
ARCHAEOLOGICAL
Dimensions: remains 25 x 7m
(82 x 30ft)
Lost: presumed 18th - 20th centuries

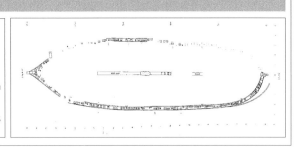

Throughout the nineteenth century the stormy North East Coast took a yearly toll of dozens of ships and men. These shipwrecks rarely made national headlines. They did not have the popular appeal of colourful heroes like Admiral Clowdisley Shovell or the romantic and valuable cargoes carried by *Colossus*. The casualties principally came from the collier fleets which toiled south from the coal staithes in the rivers Tweed, Blyth, Tyne, Wear, Tees and Esk.

Most ships were lost near the shore. As the ships grounded on sandbanks their crews scrambled into the rigging or took to boats only to be pitched into tumultous breaking seas. These tragedies were within earshot and, if darkness, rain and fog permitted, sight of friends and family helpless on the beaches. They sparked local action. Long before the RNLI existed, South Shields established a lifeboat station. Neighbouring ports followed their example and purchased Greathead lifeboats. Today, *Zetland* (1802), the oldest lifeboat in the world can be seen at Redcar on the south side of the Tees Estuary.

Across the estuary at Seaton Carew is a small ship of the very sort that the heroic *Zetland* crew would once have rowed to assist. In 1997 it became the first designated Historic Wreck between Shetland and Suffolk. The discovery and treatment of the Seaton Carew ship stems entirely from its being found on a beach where local people were able to organise a rapid response.

A September storm in 1996 had stripped sand from the beach to reveal the lower portion of the hull, apparently upright, close to low water. Its size and strong construction immediately suggested that it might be one of the local ships which carried coal. In the early eighteenth century East Coast shipbuilders began producing robust ships which combined the ability to carry heavy, bulky cargoes with sailing qualities equal to the harsh North Sea. Their excellence was immortalised when Captain Cook chose *Endeavour*, a collier from his home town of Whitby. The term 'Whitby cat' or 'North East cat' and 'collier brig' are popular synonyms for north-east merchant ships built for coal and other

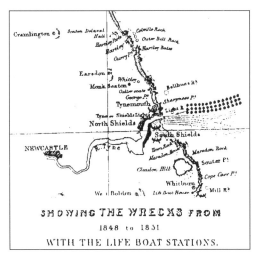

SHOWING THE WRECKS FROM
1848 to 1851
WITH THE LIFE BOAT STATIONS.

bulk trades. The three-masted, bark-rigged cats carried 400-600 tons. The later brigs, with only two masts, were smaller, some 65-95ft (20-29m) long carrying 100-200 tons.

Tees Archaeology have taken a lead in recording shipwrecks and other maritime sites such as fishing facilities and small harbours. When the Seaton Carew ship was reported, they used their Rapid Response Register to contact volunteers from the Nautical Archaeology Society to produce the first record of the ship. This action was vital as the sea once again covered the hull with over three metres of sand before official designation was in force.

The surviving hull includes 91 starboard and 71 port frames. Although the frames stood to a maximum of 1.5m (5ft) above the sand, they had been uniformly cut off, perhaps at a former beach level. It may, of course, be a redundant vessel beached for dismantling rather than a dramatic wreck. The planks, frames and ceiling are in good condition and even carved draught marks survive on the sternpost. The keelson has steps for two masts, suggesting she was a brig.

The emergence of the Seaton Carew ship is not unique. In 1996 a group of hulks was also uncovered at Mablethorpe, Lincolnshire. These have now been recorded with assistance from the Environment Agency. Much earlier examples include: in 1968 a wreck 63ft (19.2m) long with ribs each 20ft (6.1m) long uncovered at Blyth; and in 1979 a 21.3 x 4.3m (70 x 14ft) section of a ship's bottom exposed at Whitby. A countrywide mechanism for rapid response is needed. It is essential that quality records are made no matter how unexpected or transitory the opportunity for survey. This will allow objective comparisons to be made so that only the most worthwhile sites receive long-term protection.

Frank Meadow Sutcliffe photographed the brig Mary & Agnes *ashore in 1885. Opportunities to survey the remains of such wrecks on Britain's beaches have been missed, while in Holland and Poland British colliers have been recorded on the seabed.*

Viewpoint: east side of car park adjacent to Seaton Carew Golf Club
Interpretation: Hartlepool Borough Council plan a temporary exhibition and a special leaflet

Pwll Fanog (see Colour Plate 11)
Menai Strait, Gwynedd

General Location: SH 5342 7070
Protection: 53° 12.77'N 04° 11.72'W, 150m radius

ARCHAEOLOGICAL

Dimensions: estimated 56 x 22ft (17 x 6.7m)
Cargo: slates

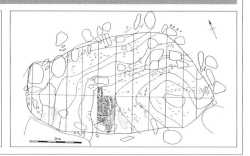

Coal is not the only mineral which filled the holds of British ships. In the 1880s slate was judged the third most important mineral after coal and iron. For the people of North West Wales the slate quarries were as potent a force in the economy, culture and landscape as the coal mines of South Wales, North East England and Lowland Scotland. From the eighteenth century Snowdonia was dominated by three major quarries which shipped their slates worldwide, from Carmarthen on the Menai Straits and Porthmadog on the Lleyn Peninsula.

The Industrial Revolution spawned towns whose buildings demanded slate. This was the force behind the 'industrialisation' of slate quarrying from the mid-eighteenth century. This market enabled land-owning families and companies to invest in technology for cutting slates and for transporting them quickly to the ports. Small harbours like Port Dinorwic were built by the slate companies.

The Pwll Fanog shipwreck belongs to the pre-industrial era of slate quarrying and transport. Slate quarrying had, like coal and tin mining, been an agrarian activity with farmers or tenants working part-time on surface outcrops of slate. Many will only have supplied local needs but there were certainly buyers further afield. Edward I had ships especially built to carry slate and other materials for the castles which he built along the Welsh coast in the thirteenth century.

In 1976 Cecil Jones was laying a trail for sport divers interested in marine biology. In the Menai Strait's notorious gloom he spotted a stack of slates whose main interest was the luxuriant colonising marine life. A couple were popped in his 'goodie bag' for a closer look in the laboratory. Soon it was the slates themselves which roused his curiosity.

Careful scrutiny of the neatly stacked slates on the seabed confirmed that this was a sunken slate ship and not a lost cargo or dumped quarry rubbish. There was no matching ship loss in local records and hopes were pinned on the slates providing a date.

There is little information on the techniques used in cutting slates before 1760. However, one of the three shapes of slate from Pwll Fanog is a type called a 'single'. It comes locally from the Llanberis and Nantile area of Gwynedd and was split with a gouge rather than a broad chisel. The quality of workmanship and tool marks on the slates suggest they are of fourteenth or fifteenth century date.

From 1978 to 1981 the investigation focused on the wreck. The slate mound is 9.9m x 5.5m (32 x 18ft). Taking that as the size of the hold the length and breadth of the original vessel can be estimated. A trench excavated across the mound showed the slates stacked seven deep, with larger ones in the upper layers, giving a total in excess of 40,000. They lay on a dunnage or packing of twigs. The old art of loading slate ships by hand was called 'hodding'.

The wooden structure of a ship is naturally buoyant. A badly damaged vessel can remain afloat until it is driven ashore and breaks up. In contrast the weight of slates in the Pwll Fanog hull probably took it quickly to the seabed 11m below. Here marine borers and swift currents weakened and carried away all exterior structure leaving just the mound of slates. Nothing could shift the slates themselves and pressed into the silt beneath them is the bottom of the ship: a keel, the garboard strakes which slot into it, and the second and third narrow clinker strakes. The wood is oak, the planks being cleft from tree trunks rather than sawn. No fastenings survive but depressions show the place of iron roves. Between the wood animal hair is used as waterproofing.

No positive dating has yet been found but, combined, the evidence suggests it belongs to the mid-16th century at the latest.

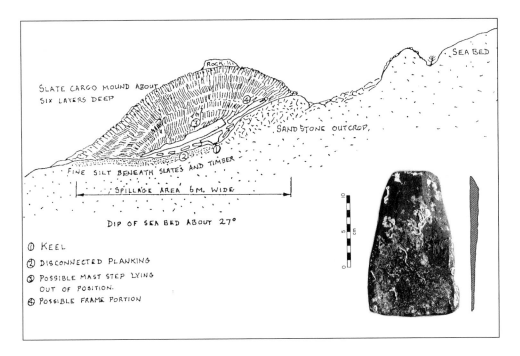

Sketch section through the cargo mound of seven layers of slate, pinning down and preserving the timbers of the hull which had heeled at 45 degrees. Inset: a slate 'single'.

Viewpoint: looking south from the Menai Bridge
Further reading: Jones, C. 1978. The Pwll Fanog Wreck – a slate cargo in the Menai Strait, *International Journal of Nautical Archaeology*, 7.2: 152-9.

Tal-y-Bont (see Colour Plate 12)
Barmouth, Dyfed

General Location: SH 5665 2229
Protection: 52° 46.73'N 04° 07.53'W, 300m radius

ARCHAEOLOGICAL

Armament: included cast & wrought-iron guns
Lost: after 1702
Voyage: probably from northern Italy
Cargo: Carrara marble

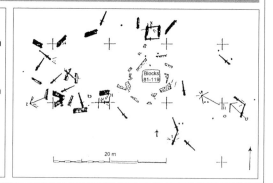

20 m

Cathedrals and stately homes appear to be far removed from the hazards of seafaring, but in the second half of the seventeenth century the Italian marble from the quarries of Carrara was being exported through Genoa and Leghorn in Dutch, English and French ships. The marble seen today by visitors to St Paul's or Blenheim Palace reached its destination, but recorded incidents and a wreck in Cardigan Bay show that this was not always so.

A treacherous reef extends from the shore near Harlech Castle and the south side of it is littered with shipwrecks. About 3km (2 miles) south of the reef in 1978 divers from Glaslyn and Harlow SACs found huge stone blocks, 'some as big as a double bed', together with cast and built-up iron guns and a bronze bell. They formed themselves into the Cae Nest Group and with the new Welsh Institute of Maritime Archaeology and History applied for site designation and a licence to survey. Sidney Wignall became project director, Haverfordwest Museum offered to conserve finds, while the Royal Armouries undertook to excavate, raise, and conserve one of the built-up guns.

Everything was in place for a long programme of survey and excavation. By 1996 there had been five seasons of survey interspersed with ten seasons of limited excavation. However, the disadvantage of slow progress is twofold. Firstly, it increases the opportunites for looters. Despite the designation order which prohibits diving within a radius of 300m, the site has been damaged, material has been stolen, but nobody has been prosecuted. Secondly, it may lower morale and make continuity, academic support and sponsorship difficult.

A book or archaeological report has yet to be published, but fortunately the finds mentioned in magazines give an idea of the potential of the site. The wreck lies in 10m on a sandy bottom with the position of anchors showing that she was trying to run ashore when she hit an isolated patch of boulders. The main cargo lay amidships, stowed in huge stacks. It comprised at least 43 blocks of Carrara marble, ranging from 80cm (31in) cubes to blocks 2.8 x 1 x 0.8m (9 x 3 x 2½ft). No fewer than 18 main battery and 8 smaller cast-iron guns and about 10 wrought-iron guns were visible. A bronze bell with the date 1677 gave the site its nickname of 'Bronze Bell Wreck'. Christian motifs and inscription led to speculation that this was actually a church bell.

A stack of pewter concreted to one of the main guns included a platter shaped like a cardinal's hat stamped in Lyon in 1700. Added to this many seventeenth-century French coins had previously been found on the beach nearby and the main armament is also probably French. Among coins from ten countries the latest dated 1702 narrowed the period of loss. Initially the idea that she was a French trader lost c.1703 conflicted with the presence of the wrought-iron swivel guns which were considered to be fifteenth century. Research triggered by the Tal-y-Bont guns has found that as late as 1700 such guns were being manfuctured in North Italy for use by merchantmen – and this is where the marble cargo certainly came from.

Other finds are navigational dividers, a purse, fine cutlery, a dental plate, a seal and remains of pistols and a rapier. A gunner's rule and a piece of wood trapped under one of the main guns showed that the site had not been long exposed and that more finds and parts of the ship might be preserved below the sand and main cargo. Trial holes showed that there was little depth above the underlying stratum of clay.

The weight of the marble blocks, calculated as about 66 tonnes, suggests she was not a large vessel. In 1689, a French flyboat was captured with 75 tons of Carrara marble. Christopher Wren, still rebuilding St Paul's Cathedral after the Fire of London, had to go down to Topsham to inspect it. He valued the marble at £1014 and it was impounded. As late as 1710 the Cathedral Commissioners were buying marble throughout Europe.

The Tal-y-Bont ship may have been a similar French vessel blown off course. However, the fate of ships was often so complex that it is difficult to unravel their full story from seabed finds. For example, an English ship carrying marble was captured by the corsair Rais Mohammed El Tadj in 1683, only to be captured in turn by a French warship. The reason for the Tal-y-Bont heavy guns is all to clear.

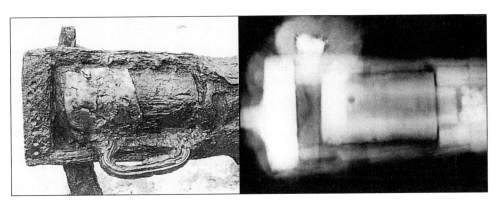

The recovered gun could be seen to be ready for firing with the touch-hole of its breech covered by a lead apron. A radiograph revealed what was inside - it could not therefore, be explained as an old gun carried as ballast.

Viewpoint: the wreck lies offshore. It is indicated by a notice on the beach to the right of the track from Dyffryn

Display: Dolgellau Record Office in summer

Further reading: Illsley, I. 1982. Admiral Lord Edward Russell and the building of St Paul's Cathedral. *Mariner's Mirror*, 68: 305-5

Reusable Containers

From the sixteenth to eighteenth centuries salt-glazed stoneware is the most common pottery on wrecks of European nationality. There is a good reason for this. When the clay was fired to about 1250°C it became strong and impervious. From documents and finds we know that stonewares were made in the Rhineland and exported on a huge scale. For instance, during 1615 the equivalent of 320,000 quart jugs are recorded as being landed in London alone. Although no cargo of these has yet been found on a shipwreck, they are found used as containers.

Their robustness, and the near-spherical form and small necks of the jugs, made them ideal for the safe transport at sea of precious commodities, such as medicines and mercury. Mercury was found to be still inside a Bellarmine jug on *Kennemerland* wrecked in 1664 and fruit remains were found in another from the site. If the containers were protected in wickerwork they could survive numerous voyages to all parts of the world. Veteran Frechen Bellarmine jugs as much as thirty years old have been found on a Dutch East Indiaman wrecked off Western Australia while the Raeren jugs in a medicine chest on *Mary Rose* had been in use even longer.

Sherds of stoneware are commonly found on land sites. The many forms and designs were taken to represent a linear development. This chronology has been blown apart by shipwrecks containing many forms which had clearly been used contemporaneously. These wrecks have incidentally pushed back the date for stoneware manufacture in Britain to about 1630. For shipwrecks themselves, closer dating evidence may be provided by fragile pottery and cargoes of ceramics.

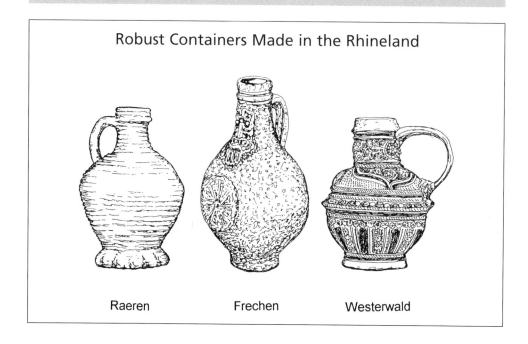

Robust Containers Made in the Rhineland

Raeren   Frechen   Westerwald

11 A World-wide Fleet

HMS *Victory* (1765) is our memorial to the eighteenth-century navy. She embodies the ships and men deployed in a world-wide strategy which prevented a single country, whether Spain or France, becoming all-powerful in Europe. By close blockade they held enemy ships in harbour and prevented imports of goods and bullion. By combined operations in Europe and in colonial territories, from the Americas to the East Indies, they diverted resources from the enemy's armies in Europe

As a 1st Rate *Victory* represents the largest but least numerous naval ships; fewer than twenty 100-gun ships were built between 1678 and 1815. In contrast none of the 2nd or very numerous 3rd Rates survive. Too small to stand in the line 4th & 5th Rates, or frigates, were the 'eyes and ears of the fleet'. They kept watch on enemy movements, relayed messages and ran special errands such as conveying VIPs or intercepting privateers. Two are still afloat, but both post-date the great victory at Trafalgar in 1805: *Trincomalee* (1817) and *Unicorn* (1824).

Victory, *Unicorn* and *Trincomalee* had long service lives. Repairs and then ongoing restoration of necessity diminishes the proportion of original structure, fittings and equipment. Curators rely on documents to tell them how their ship should look, but they can also turn to archaeology. Five ships in four Historic Wreck Sites date to this period, three English and two French-built. They were not lost in action but through failure of gear, wildness of weather and misjudged navigation. This was typical. Between 1793 and 1815 fewer than a dozen naval ships were sunk by the enemy but the sea took over 300.

Tearing Ledge
Western Rocks, Isle of Scilly

General Location: SV 8093 0618
Protection: 49° 52' 12"N 06° 26' 29"W,
200m radius
ARCHAEOLOGICAL
Lost: artefacts date to 1707 disaster
Armament: included iron cannon

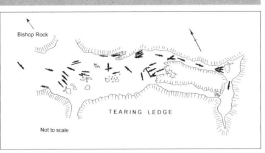

Bishop Rock

TEARING LEDGE

Not to scale

On 22 October 1707 the lives of 1684 men were lost with the four ships *Association, Eagle, Romney* and *Firebrand*. Admiral Clowdisley Shovell had faced the problem of any mariner entering the English Channel before longitude could be accurately measured. A course had to be set through the Western Approaches to clear the Lizard, keep off the French coast and avoid the Isles of Scillies, 147 low-lying rocks and islands spread over 180 square kilometres (70 sq miles). Shovell miscalculated. A contemporary chart by Gostelo shows the ships wrecked on the Western Rocks, with the 4th Rate *Romney* on Tearing Ledge.

In the 1960s the Ministry of Defence gave salvage contracts to at least three diving groups who were hunting for *Association* and the bullion she carried. She was found in 1967 and salvaged commercially. In the 1980s visiting divers were still finding about 2000 coins each year. Iron guns were also found on Tearing Ledge and the Crim, and *Firebrand* was located.

The identity of the Tearing Ledge site is contentious. Most arguments centre on how to tally the number and size of guns found on the seabed with those believed to be aboard either *Romney* or *Eagle*. *Romney* was a 5th Rate built at Blackwall on the Thames in 1694. *Eagle* was a 3rd Rate built as part of the Thirty Ships programme in 1679. Objects from the Tearing Ledge site are displayed in Hastings Shipwreck Heritage Centre to show the sort of things which might be found inside *Anne*. They include parts of a copper kettle, pewter tableware, buckles, shot and cannon balls.

Roland Morris agreed with documentary evidence that *Romney* was on Tearing Ledge, as he believed the guns on the Crim tallied with those left aboard *Eagle* after she had put some ashore in the Mediterranean. He modelled the striking of *Eagle* on the rock and the movement of the hull to its final sinking position to account for guns in three locations.

Peter McBride, Richard Larn and Rex Cowan, who investigated the site after it was designated, favoured it as *Eagle*, believing there to be too many guns for *Romney*.

The salvage and sale of artefacts from the *Association* and other sites was highly controversial. It fuelled the lobby which led to the Protection of Wrecks Act (1973). A visit to St Mary's Museum and Penzance Maritime Museum shows the quality of material from the Shovell wrecks. There is bronze and iron ordnance, navigational instruments, fine tableware, personal items and ships fittings, and it includes metals, ceramics and wood. That only one of the wrecks should have been designated contrasts with the Great Storm Wrecks on the Goodwin Sands.

In November 1973 some Scillonians proposed forming the Isles of Scilly Oceanic Trust to take responsibility for managing both the shipwrecks and the marine flora and fauna. Trustees were to include representatives from the Duchy of Cornwall, Nature Conservancy and museums, with a committee comprising local representatives of BSAC and Sea Fisheries Committees. They had already seen the shortcoming of the new Protection of Wrecks Act in not providing visitor access. Unfortunately they were years ahead of their time. Statutory Marine Nature Reserves only came into being in 1981. So far the management of Historic Wrecks within Marine Nature Reserves has not been formally integrated as part of the Reserves' management responsibilities.

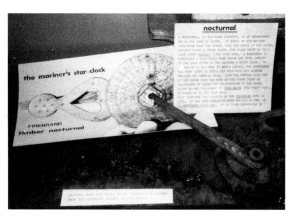

Nocturnal on display in Penzance Maritime Museum. It was recovered from Firebrand, *one of four Clowdisley Shovell shipwrecks discovered, of which only Tearing Ledge has been designated.*

The sale of historic objects from wrecks is controversial. As artefacts they are three-dimensional documents containing vital information about the past. As works of art or costly materials they have a monetary value. Once dispersed objects can be hard to trace. For this reason, it is vital that they are thoroughly recorded and researched if they are to be sold.

Viewpoint: The Rocks are now marked by the Bishop Rock Lighthouse, the destination of fair-weather boat trips from St Mary's which is about 11km (7 miles) away.
Display: Penzance Maritime Museum; Hastings Shipwreck Heritage Centre
Further reading: Larn, R. 1974. *Shipwrecks of the Isles of Scilly*

Colossus (see Colour Plate 15)
Isles of Scilly, Cornwall

General Location: SV 8778 1144

Protection: REVOKED 49° 55.15'N 06° 21.02'W, 300m radius

HISTORICAL

Built: 1787, Gravesend. Clevely

Type: 3rd Rate

Dimensions: 172ft gun deck x 48ft (52.5 x 14.6m)

Armament: 74 guns

Lost: 11 December 1798

Voyage: Naples to Portsmouth **Cargo:** spoils of war; wounded; Hamilton Collection

Complement: crew plus 200 wounded **Saved:** all bar one

Site chart of *Colossus*

On 1 August 1798 British fortunes in the war against Napoleon were boosted when Nelson defeated the French fleet in the Battle of the Nile, at Aboukir Bay. The 3rd Rate *Colossus* had been badly damaged a year earlier and was now carrying stores for Nelson's fleet. Her holds were emptied to repair the battered English ships which limped into the shelter of Naples. The spoils from the battle were then loaded. In addition eight boxes were stowed which contained antiquities – elegant vases – collected by Sir William Hamilton. Nelson, lover of Hamilton's wife Emma, had promised them safe carriage. Above the holds over 200 sick and wounded seamen were laid in the dark orlop deck. They were hopeful of swift passage to England but *Colossus* sailed with orders to call at Lisbon for cochineal, specie and other goods.

On display in Penzance Maritime Museum some of the many artefacts and fittings for which the Colossus site was not designated.

Colossus reached the Isles of Scilly in the easterly winds of December. Taking every precaution, Captain Murray anchored in St Mary's Sound to await favourable winds. By the 10th the wind had become a gale which parted the anchor cable. It was too dark to find a route to the safety of open sea and Murray could only wait as his ship dragged her remaining anchors. The wind veered to the south and the Sound became like a funnel through which the storm rushed. By 4am *Colossus* was aground on Southward Well Reef. Lying to the south of Samson Island it is overlooked from the battery on St Mary's Island but in the wild night no assistance could be hoped for. With water reaching the upper deck gun ports the wounded were lashed into the rigging. Evacuation began at 8am and all but one were saved.

Colossus lay on her beam ends, her deck towards the beach and her stern to the east. Salvage, official and illicit, carried on for more than a year as the sea slowly destroyed the hull.

Roland Morris longed to find Hamilton's vases. His search for *Colossus* began decades before anyone thought of protecting historic wreck sites. As a salvage diver in the days of hard helmets and lead boots he first searched Southward Well Reef in 1939. It was thirty-five years later when his team, with the freedom of SCUBA, finally located her.

Morris wrote gripping descriptions of the powerful seas striking the West Country. For him it was nonsense to propose applying theories of archaeological stratigraphy and distribution to the seabed.

Despite these beliefs Morris carefully studied the account of her loss and the original ship plans. He knew that the seabed scatter of objects in some way still related to the sailing *Colossus*. Discovery of the bower anchors, with shanks pointing in the direction which the ship dragged, led onto the main site. Bottles, pins, ship's pottery, and most importantly, copper hull rivets were enough for seasoned wreck hunters. The bow position was marked by bricks from the galley. Over 200m away, more than three times the ship's original length, rudder pintles marked the stern.

The seabed was rock, broken by sand-filled gullies in which small objects were trapped. Morris focused his search by measuring the distance from stern and bow to the hold containing the Hamilton vases. His deduction was right and the chosen gully produced the first precious sherd of decorated pottery. The British Museum confirmed its identity and supported plans for recovery.

The Protection of Wrecks Act had just become law. The team diving the 'Big C', as *Colossus* was affectionately known, saw it as a means to keep 'cowboy' divers off their site. It was designated on the artistic and archaeological merit of its cargo, with an understanding that designation would only stand while the pottery sherds were recovered.

Morris' published comments make clear his view of the conditions imposed: what purpose could survey serve on a seabed which continually moved? and how could a non-diving specialist in classical pottery supervise underwater salvage? The lack of empathy between divers and museum staff, as Morris reports, was clearly strengthened by the lack of interest in the ship and nautical artefacts.

Viewpoint: St Mary's Garrison overlooks the wreck site on Samson Island
Display: Penzance Maritime Museum; St Mary's Museum (a few objects)
Further reading: Morris, R. 1979. *HMS Colossus*

Hamilton's Greek Collection

Greek settlement of southern Italy was well established by the fifth-sixth centuries BC and the wealthiest colonists purchased fine tableware exported from the homeland. This had beautifully painted decoration of animals and figures, either in red on a burnished black ground, 'red figure', or black figures on a red ground, 'black figure'. These pot paintings are full of information on all aspects of Greek life and Greek art. The finest are true masterpieces.

While Sir William Hamilton was resident in Naples he used every opportunity to add to his collection of antiquities and 'Etruscan vases', as they were then called. Large numbers were being recovered by tomb robbers and Sir William was well placed to acquire the finest specimens. In 1772 he sold his first collection for the then huge sum of 8000 guineas to the British Museum. There it exerted a far-reaching influence on art and fashion, inspiring, for instance, Wedgwood's 'Etruscan wares'. To Hamilton the loss of a third of his second collection in *Colossus* was a great blow. Two hundred years later the careful record drawings which he had commissioned in Italy enabled sherds recovered from the wreck to be assigned to individual vases.

Antiquarianism in action: Emma Hamilton, wearing a splendid hat, watches the opening of a Greek grave as her husband, Sir William, clasps the latest addition to his collection.

Assurance/Pomone (see Colour Plate 16)
The Needles, Isle of Wight

General Location: SZ 2892 8481
Protection: 50° 39′ 42″N 01° 35′ 27″W, 75m radius

HISTORICAL

Built: 1747, Bursledon / 1805, Frindsbury
Type: 5th Rate frigate / 5th Rate frigate
Dimensions: 133 x 38ft (40.5 x 11.6m) / 150 x 40ft (45.7 x 12.2m)
Armament: 44 guns / 38 guns
Lost: 24 April 1753/ 14 October 1811
Voyage: Jamaica to Portsmouth / Constantinople to Portsmouth
Carrying: Governor of Jamaica / Ambassador to Persia

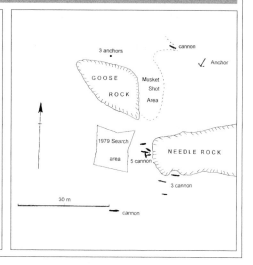

Running a typical frigate errand, the 5th Rate *Assurance* was carrying the Governor of Jamaica home to Portsmouth when she struck a submerged rock close to the Needles. The site was found in 1970 by Derek Williams who had researched the ship. However, when John Bingeman became involved, in 1978, he realised that it was not one but two, or more, wreck sites.

The Needles is an accident black spot. A shifting sandbank forces ships entering the Solent close to the Needles where there are a number of submerged rocks. *Assurance* hit Goose Rock in 1753. In 1811 the 5th Rate *Pomone* hit the same rock, and in 1837 the schooner *Dream* was also lost there. Their wooden hulls do not survive on the bare chalk seabed. Copper fastenings, fragments of sheathing and small artefacts, such as musket shot and coins and buttons, are found in the fissures and gullies where they are rolled by the powerful tides and waves.

Seabed investigation focused first on the guns. Their positions suggested that material from *Assurance* lay to the north of the site and from *Pomone* to the south. By 1985 over 3500 finds had been raised and then catalogued by Paul Simpson working for the Isle of Wight Archaeological Unit. Most artefacts represented only the inorganic components of shipboard equipment. Thus the bilge pump consisted only of its chains and metal fittings. However, some organic material did survive sealed in concretion, for example grains of wheat. Historic records and the surviving *Trincomalee* helped to link many objects with *Pomone*. Careful recording showed that their seabed positions were not random. This suggestion went against not only the views of seasoned divers but evolving archaeological theory.

In the early 1980s the National Maritime Museum still had an Archaeological Research Centre. A member of staff, Keith Muckelroy, had studied the existing historic wrecks and devised a grading system. This ranged from those with preservative environments, such as mud or sand which could engulf a whole hull, to those, like the Needles, where a ship would break up, organic material disintegrate and no coherent pattern remain.

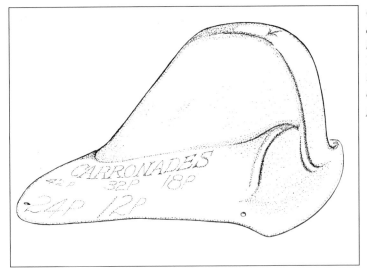

Guns were kept loaded and ready to fire. This lead apron recovered from Pomone *once fitted over the flintlock of a carronade to keep the powder dry.*

Two carronades from Pomone. On is still covered in concretion while the other has been conserved ready for display in Portsmouth Historic Dockyard.

David Tomalin, the Isle of Wight Archaeological Officer, hoped that analysis of the *Pomone* site would throw light on the debate between those who advocate applying the strictest archaeological techniques to seabed sites and those who believe that the mobility of the environment makes the effort unwarranted. He wanted a comprehensive topographical survey of the site to check the artefact distributions. For a dozen seasons the survey has waited on the right combination of manpower, high-tech equipment and luck with weather and tides.

In 1997 the Hampshire & Wight Trust for Maritime Archaeology secured the help of Submetrix, designers and builders of sonar systems. They surveyed the site using ISIS 100 which offered a twofold advantage. Firstly it covers wide swathes, up to fifteen times the water depth, so a survey can be completed quickly even in shallow water. Secondly, it has an arc of 300 degrees so data can be collected right up to the shoreline, an important consideration for sites like the Needles.

Hopes for the *Assurance/Pomone* site are now high. The new topographical survey can be integrated with the archaeological data so the final publication can fully explain the wreck site. Options are being considered for allowing visiting divers onto the site. With the Needles a major tourist attraction, discussion includes creating close-circuit television links so that the underwater site can be viewed from the land.

Tiny South American silver scent bottle, probably being brought home by Mrs Trelawney aboard Assurance.

The wheel from one of Pomone's *blocks, marked with the broad arrow and the maker's initials, Walter Taylor of Southampton.*

Viewpoint: the Needles Battery, opened by the National Trust, overlooks the site, as do the access paths

Display: Portsmouth Historic Dockyard (external display case and carronade). Collections: Isle of Wight County Council

Further reading: Bingeman, J. 1989. Gunlocks: their introduction to the Navy. In Smith, D. (ed.) *British Naval Armament*. Royal Armouries Conference Proceedings

Hazardous
Bracklesham Bay, West Sussex

General Location: SZ 8056 9536

Protection: 50° 45.10'N 00° 51.47'W, 100m radius

HISTORICAL

Built: 1698, Port Louis, France

Type: French 3rd Rate changed to English 4th Rate

Dimensions: 137 x 38ft (41.8x11.6m) as built   **Armament:** 54 guns

Rebuilt: 1704 Portsmouth

Lost: November 1706   **Voyage:** Plymouth to the Downs   **Complement:** 320

Hazardous was found by chance. Several fishermen and divers had recovered isolated guns from Bracklesham Bay before divers came across the wreck in 7m of water. Their discovery, in 1977, was followed by periodic visits but urgent investigation and designation only began after the seabed dropped in 1984. The cause of the erosion is not known but it may be a knock-on from nearby sea defence works. The excellent state of exposed timbers shows that the wreck was previously safely buried rather than periodically exposed.

Matches with the pewter tableware and navigational dividers from *Dartmouth*, lost in 1690, gave the clue to the wreck's identity. *Hazardous* was the only documented naval loss off Bracklesham in the same era.

In the poor November weather of 1706 HMS *Hazardous* was en route from Dartmouth to the Downs following the superior officer in *Advice*. Running for shelter in the Solent *Advice* failed to signal *Hazardous* that they were entering shoal water. By the time Lieutenant John Hare realised his position he was unable to turn his ship to safety. After the anchor failed to hold his best option was to run *Hazardous* ashore in an attempt to save ship and crew. Unfortunately, with the ship in the surf zone, it proved impossible to salvage all of the guns let alone the hull. Study of the seabed has now shown why.

The site is in some ways similar to *Dartmouth*. It seems that as *Hazardous* drove ashore she grounded on a small reef, perhaps overlain by sand. This broke her back. The bow section settled into the silt on the shore side of the reef, where the

Diver Prosecution

The *Hazardous* was the first site on which divers were prosecuted for illegally diving an Historic Wreck. Four men were each fined £125 plus £275 costs.

Diver Magazine reported their defence, pointing to the wreck being inadequately marked, lacking the regulation 1m-high buoy with the words 'Historic Wreck'. In addition the shoreside warning was only an A4 size notice on the wall of a public toilet.

Today the toilet carries one of the few interpretation boards erected by the then Department of National Heritage. It is positioned in a public car park from which visitors can see the site.

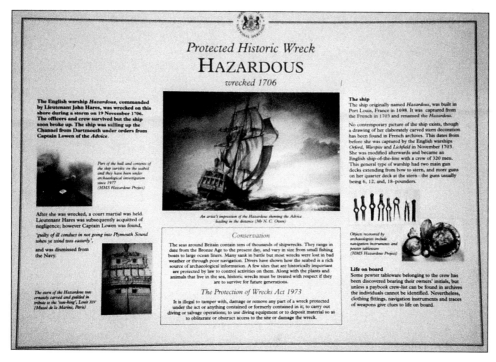

Protected Historic Wreck

HAZARDOUS

wrecked 1706

The English warship *Hazardous*, commanded by Lieutenant John Hares, was wrecked on this shore during a storm on 19 November 1706. The officers and crew survived but the ship soon broke up. The ship was sailing up the Channel from Dartmouth under orders from Captain Lowen of the *Advice*.

Part of the hull and contents of the ship survive on the seabed and they have been under archaeological investigation since 1977 (HMS Hazardous Project)

After she was wrecked, a court martial was held. Lieutenant Hares was subsequently acquitted of negligence; however Captain Lowen was found, 'guilty of ill conduct in not going into Plymouth Sound when ye wind was easterly', and was dismissed from the Navy.

The stern of the Hazardous was ornately carved and guilded in tribute to the 'sun-king', Louis XIV (Musée de la Marine, Paris)

The ship
The ship originally named *Hazardeux*, was built in Port Louis, France in 1698. It was captured from the French in 1703 and renamed the *Hazardous*.

No contemporary picture of the ship exists, though a drawing of her elaborately carved stern decoration has been found in French archives. This dates from before she was captured by the English warships *Oxford*, *Warspite* and *Lichfield* in November 1703. She was modified afterwards and became an English ship-of-the-line with a crew of 320 men. This general type of warship had two main gun decks extending from bow to stern, and more guns on her quarter deck at the stern—the guns usually being 6, 12, and, 18-pounders.

An artist's impression of the Hazardous showing the Advice leading in the distance (Mr N. C. Owen)

Conservation
The seas around Britain contain tens of thousands of shipwrecks. They range in date from the Bronze Age to the present day, and vary in size from small fishing boats to large ocean liners. Many sank in battle but most wrecks were lost in bad weather or through poor navigation. Divers have shown how the seabed is a rich source of archaeological information. A few sites that are historically important are protected by law to control activities on them. Along with the plants and animals that live in the sea, historic wrecks must be treated with respect if they are to survive for future generations.

The Protection of Wrecks Act 1973
It is illegal to tamper with, damage or remove any part of a wreck protected under the act or anything contained or formerly contained in it; to carry out diving or salvage operations; to use diving equipment or to deposit material so as to obliterate or obstruct access to the site or damage the wreck.

Objects recovered by archaeologists include navigation instruments and pewter tableware (HMS Hazardous Project)

Life on board
Some pewter tableware belonging to the crew has been discovered bearing their owners' initials, but unless a paybook crew-list can be found in archives the individuals cannot be identified. Nevertheless, clothing fittings, navigation instruments and traces of weapons give clues to life on board.

Many of the Historic Wreck sites are easily seen from the promenades and car parks of seaside resorts or from coastal paths. Hazardous *is one of the few to have an interpretation board.*

stem and port side are now preserved. The stern slewed around allowing some of its contents to scatter. The stern itself was weighed down by guns and so preserved. Whereas artefacts on *Dartmouth* correspond with their original positions in the hull there is mixing on the *Hazardous* site.

Hazardous was not English. She was launched from Port Louis in 1698 for the French Navy as *Le Hazardeux*. Whilst on loan to a French privateer in 1703 she was captured by ships under Admiral Clowdisley Shovell. She had resisted for six hours and was towed to Portsmouth 'a perfect wreck' where she was rebuilt. The rebuild changed her from a French 3rd Rate of 50 guns to an English 4th Rate of 54 guns. Details of construction recorded on the seabed show that she retained distinctive French features. Her frames are set in pairs bolted together longitudinally. In the bow the frames are set at increasing angles. These so-called cant frames were not introduced into English warships until about 1715. The site is littered with scraps of lead and this has been found driven between the planking as caulking. Only two parallels have been found for using lead in this way. The wreck of a 16th-century Spanish ship, *San Esteban*, and a description for building an 80-gun ship in the 1690s. No parallel has been found for her other characteristic. A material which is probably a lead alloy has been placed between the components of her laminated bow structure during construction. Presumably it deterred the dreaded ship worm.

Viewpoint: the wreck lies 800m south-east of the public slipway by the seafront car park at Bracklesham Bay

Further reading: Owen, N. 1991. Hazardous 1990-1991 interim report. *International Journal of Nautical Archaeology*, 20.4: 325-34

Invincible (see Colour Plate 14)
Horse Tail Sand, Hampshire

General Location: SZ 6793 9377
Protection: 50° 44.34'N 01° 02.2'W, 100m radius

HISTORICAL

Built: 1744, Rochefort, France
Type: 3rd Rate

Dimensions: 172 x 48ft (51 x 14.9m)
Armament: 74 guns
Lost: 22 February 1758
Voyage: St Helens, Louisberg
Complement: 700
Saved: All

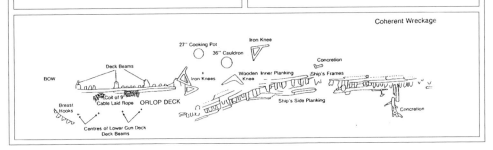

The increase in the French navy in the 1670s had prompted Pepys' innovatory construction of standard size ships, 1st, 2nd and 3rd Rates. During the many conflicts of the eighteenth century the 3rd Rates developed as the most versatile of warships. By 1805, the year of the Battle of Trafalgar, the British navy included 87 of these 74-gun ships. While earlier ships had carried 74 guns these so-called 'true 74s' followed French initiatives. In *Magnanime* and *Invincible* they established the form of the 'true 74'. *Invincible* was launched from Rochefort in 1744.

Invincible was a new design suited to a world-wide fleet. It was no longer enough for the French navy to challenge British dominance in the Channel; ships were needed to convoy merchantmen and support military actions from the Americas to the East Indies. Large 1st and 2nd Rates were expensive to build and arm, and, as high three-deckers, they could be slow and unwieldy sailers. *Invincible* was given a longer hull than earlier 3rd Rates which allowed all her guns to be ranged along two decks: twenty-eight 36-pounders on the lower; thirty 18-pounders on the upper; and sixteen 8-pounders on the forecastle and quarterdeck. She combined immense fire-power with a low hull making her stable and seakindly.

Invincible was captured by the English fleet under Admiral Anson at the First Battle of Finisterre on 3 May 1747. In his despatches Anson, who later became a great reformer of the navy, made comparison between *Invincible* and his flagship. *Invincible*'s gundeck was wider and more than 7ft (2m) longer than that of his 90-gun three-decker, while an English 3rd Rate carrying 70 guns measured only about 160ft (48.8m) in length.

A series of mishaps caused the loss of *Invincible* as she attempted to leave St Helens Roads with a fleet bound for Louisberg in 1758. Her anchor would not come clear of the bottom and then, when hauled to the surface, it fouled her bow and could not be 'catted' (secured). Time could not be given to the problem as *Invincible* was falling behind the main fleet. She started north-east across the Solent in order to tack to clear Bembridge Ledges. As she turned the rudder jammed and the wind pushed her aground on Horse Tail Sand. She soon began to leak. For three days vigorous efforts were made to free her including lightening the ship by taking out all the guns. It proved impossible and she toppled onto h[...]

Her wreck was found in 1979. Arthur Mack caught his fishing nets on [...] which he later searched for and asked John Broomhead and Jim Boyle to d[...] on John Bingeman to organise an archaeological investigation. Initially h[...] uncertain as shot sizes did not match the ordnance list but, later, som[...] [...] discovered which ordered a change in armament. Her identity was beyond dispute when divers found a leather sail marker carrying her name.

The sands have provided excellent protection and *Invincible* is to the eighteenth century what *Mary Rose* is to the Tudor period. The surviving hull structure is thought to be three times as large as the recovered portion of *Mary Rose*. Although the construction and career of *Invincible* is well-documented excavation of the hull still produced new information. For example, she has iron knees (structural brackets).

A multitude of objects of all materials and uses have been found inside the hull. These have been used to enrich understanding of eighteenth-century shipboard life as replicas have been used on *Victory*, on the copy of *Endeavour* and for a new BBC film 'Hornblower'. The many finds needed conservation and an attempt to recoup this and project costs was made by auctioning some artefacts. This was controversial. Many people feel that collections from archaeological sites should be kept together for future reference. There was also unease that this signified approval of commercial salvage from historic wrecks. On the other hand there were few funding options available. There were many duplicate artefacts and a number of museums across the world made acquisitions. These can be used to interpret contemporary shipwrecks or historical events from which there are no surviving remains.

Since excavation stopped the site has been monitored by divers despite sewage from an outfall constructed in 1991 only 1300m away. In November 1997 the MV *Amer VED* went aground within the protected area. Divers noted that she had damaged the wreck over 20m of its length. Using for comparison a 1995 remote sensing survey, a Chirp sub-bottom survey by the University of Southampton confirmed, with great accuracy, the extent of the damage. Such methods provide an option for site monitoring in areas which are hazardous for divers.

Mess tables on Endeavour *set with replicas of utensils from* Invincible *(pl.14)*

Viewpoint: there is an interpretation panel close to Southsea Castle with views out to Dean Sand
Display: Chatham Historic Dockyard; Royal Naval Museum, Portsmouth; other maritime and ordnance museums
Further reading: Lavery, B. 1987. *The Royal Navy's First Invincible*

A stave-built tub from Invincible. *It shows the exceptional preservation of organic materials, wood and rope, which are rarely found in the dry conditions of land sites.*

12 Adopting Innovation

The wreck of Brunel's *SS Great Britain* (1843) was brought home to Bristol from the Falklands. Now restored, she symbolises the revolution in shipbuilding made possible by iron frames and plates and steam power. Traditional wooden hulls were heavy and their length limited by stresses on timbers joined longitudinally. The strength of iron enabled hulls to be made larger and lighter so increasing their cargo capacity. Time in port, becalmed, or off-course costs money. While initially unreliable, engines eventually countered these difficulties by providing swifter passages and regular schedules. By pioneering the new technology of shipbuilding Britain gained an economic advantage over the shipping nations of the world. It ensured her dominance throughout the nineteenth century.

Only two designated Historic Wrecks belong to this era. By coincidence one is an example of a common type of ship, the other is a unique experimental vessel. In choosing archaeological and historical monuments to preserve as illustrations of life during each phase of history a balance must be found between representing the 'everyday' and the frontier of change (even if it sometimes proved to be a blind alley).

Iona II
Lundy, Devon

General Location: SS 1508 4612
Protection: 51° 11.03'N 04° 38.78'W, 50m radius
HISTORICAL
Built: 1863 Govan, Clyde. J & T Thomson
Type: Paddle steamer passenger ferry
Dimensions: 245 x 25ft (74.5 x 7.6m)
Lost: 2 February 1864
Voyage: Clyde to America

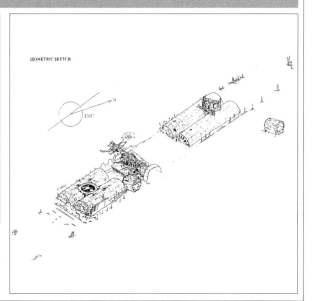

ISOMETRIC SKETCH

Isometric view of the surviving hull drawn by Carole Rule after the first licensed survey by Potters Bar SAC in 1990.

In 1989 *Iona II* brought the designation of Historic Wrecks into new waters. The wreck was a first on three counts as the ship was less than 150 years old, built of iron and powered by steam. She remains the sole representative of merchant shipping in the steam era.

Experiments with steam-driven boats took off in the late eighteenth century on the rivers of France and America. By 1802 the British had the famous *Charlotte Dundas* steaming on the Forth Clyde Canal. By 1812 the paddle steamer *Comet* was providing Europe's first regular coastal passenger service from Glasgow. Scottish expertise was probably behind the enterprising steamer service on Sweden's Gota Kanal, where the wreck of *Eric Nordewall* (1837) has survived in remarkable condition.

Initially steam engines, with huge coal consumption, could not compete economically with sail at sea. Steam ships were only used for passengers and for special cargoes with either a high profit or, like the mails, a government subsidy. From the 1880s the triple expansion engine changed everything. Its efficiency was summed up as the ability to carry a ton of cargo one mile on the coal-produced energy equivalent to burning a single sheet of quality writing paper.

Iona II, launched on the Clyde in 1863, represents the peak for mid-century passenger steamers. She was 245ft (75m) long with a beam, excluding paddle boxes, of only 25ft (7.6m). Construction in iron, which became available from the 1840s, gave longitudinal strength to withstand sagging from heavy machinery amidships and vibrations from the paddles. The tradition of Clyde passenger steamers is kept alive by the Paddle Steamer Preservation Society. Each year *Waverley* (1946) and *Balmoral* (1949) run a season of excursions.

Iona II was built for the successful Glasgow company of Hutcheson, which served the

Iona II *under steam before her passenger saloons were removed.*

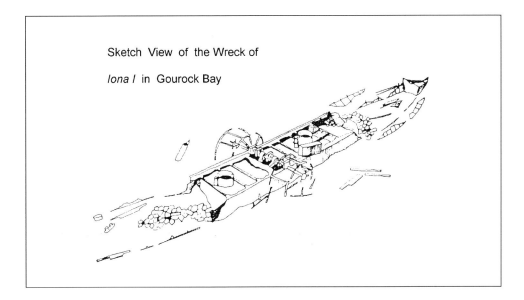

Iona *(1855) had oscillating engines. These were introduced in 1827 and became the norm for driving paddles. At the time of designation* Iona II's *oscillating engines were noted as probably unique survivors. However, a year earlier, Peter Moir in his book* Clyde Shipwrecks, *drew the wreck of* Iona *in Gourock Bay and noted 'the remaining centre section is approximately 25m long. The engines with their large brass counterweights and the boilers are the most obvious visible features ... the bases of the twin stacks are still visible.'*

Clyde Basin and Western Isles. River ferries provided everyday transport, while excursion trips boosted the development of resorts such as Rothesay and Helensburgh. The river steamers were also vital transport for workers. Services to the Western Isles enabled large numbers of crofters to find seasonal employment in the Lanarkshire cotton industry and lowland agriculture.

Iona II's sea trials were a huge success, making twenty three knots over the measured course. The newspapers were effusive in their praise of her passenger facilities 'finished in most magnificent style of art' and including a 75ft (22.9m) long dining room and a deck saloon of 180ft (54.9m). In less than a year all this luxury was to be stripped from the ship.

Across the Atlantic there was civil war. American shipowners wanted swift ships capable of breaking the blockade imposed by their adversaries. Hutcheson & Co took advantage of exceedingly high prices when they sold *Iona II*'s predecessor *Iona* (1855). At the end of her first season *Iona II* was also purchased for blockade running.

Remarkably both ships sank in British waters and the wrecks of both survive: *Iona I* in Gourock Bay after colliding with SS *Chanticleer* in 1862; *Iona II* off Lundy two years later. In 1976 *Iona II* was discovered in mud at 20m by John Shaw, while leading dive holidays. He carried out some excavation and a few objects were given to Greenock Museum. Diving guides listed the site among Lundy's wreck attractions until, following concern for her future, she was designated in 1989.

On land, heritage protection increasingly takes account of the relative merit of sites of the same type. What might be learnt about the preservation of iron ships and the management of wreck sites from an archaeological comparison of the *Iona*s?

Viewpoint: The wreck lies offshore but the site can be seen from the coastal path
Collections: McLean Museum & Art Gallery, Greenock
Further reading: Duckworth, C & Langmuir, G. 1987. *West Highland Steamers*. 2-3 (historical)

Resurgam
Rhyl, Gwynedd

General Location: Beyond conversion programme of RCAHMW

Protection: 53° 23.78'N 03° 33.18'W, 300m radius
HISTORICAL

Built: 1879 Cochrane, Birkenhead

Type: First engine-powered submarine

Dimensions: 42 x 12ft (12.8 x 3.7m)

Armament: Whitehead torpedoes

Lost: 25 February 1880

Voyage: Rhyl to Portsmouth under tow

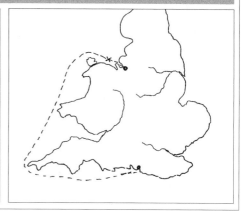

Resurgam is the only submarine designated as an Historic Wreck. She was an experimental craft built in 1879. At that time the British Admiralty could not imagine that submarines would change the character of sea warfare. In the next major European conflict, the 1914-18 War, German U-Boats destroyed 5,282 vessels (12,284,757 gross registered tonnes).

For three centuries marine salvors and visionaries in naval warfare had sought a successful submersible vessel. William Bourne, writing in 1580, had produced a feasible idea. He described how a vessel might be made to sink by using screw-controlled leather bulkheads to draw water ballast into a hull. His theories were put into practice by a Dutchman, Cornelius Van Drabbel. His remarkable vessel was demonstrated for James I by travelling submerged from Westminster to Greenwich.

From Van Drabbel's time until the end of the nineteenth century no fewer than 180 submarine designs are documented. At least fifty of these were actually built. For some unknown reason the designers were often men of the church.

In 1878 the Reverend George William Garrett designed and had built a submersible. This was only 13ft (4m) long but tests in Liverpool Docks were successful and led him to design *Resurgam*. She was built by J T Cochrane at the Britannia Ironworks in Birkenhead. Her steel hull was cylindrical with a cone-shaped bow and stern. The central section was clad in teak. A large boiler and Lamm-type engine filled nearly all of the midships section. A huge head of steam was generated prior to submerging. It gave a dive duration of some 10-12 miles (16-19km) at a speed of 2-3 knots. In 1926 one of her three-man crew recalled the extreme heat, exhaustion and painful ears experienced in an initial 30-hour dive during which there was no space to sit or lie down.

Resurgam was bound for naval trials at Portsmouth when her towing cable broke and she was lost. The British Government remained sceptical and did not fund research. Garret joined the Swedish gunmaker, Nordenfeldt, to develop his designs and three submarines were built by the Naval Construction & Armament Company of Barrow-in-Furness. Two entered the Greek & Turkish navies but with little success. The third foundered *en route* to its Russian buyers.

When the British Government finally ordered submarines they used designs from a Briton who had found backing in America. Following Garrett's lead they chose Vickers of

Contemporary photograph of the newly completed experimental submarine Resurgam.

Barrow-in-Furness to build the first five British ' Hollands'. After her service life was over, *Holland No.1,* like *Resurgam*, sank under tow. In 1981 she was raised and taken to the Royal Navy Submarine Museum, Gosport. Chemicals had been used to coat the hull after lifting and she appeared in excellent condition. Unfortunately, after a number of years, salts deep in the metal began to cause disintegration. She was transferred to a large capsule for further treatment and can only be viewed through its portholes until she becomes stable.

The search for *Resurgam* spans thirty years. In the 1960s she was described in the shipping magazine *Sea Breezes* and a yachtsman reported striking a large cylindrical object off Rhyl. On several occasions remote sensing equipment was used but without success. In the 1990s William Garrett, great grandson of the inventor, backed a high-tech survey. The final discovery was tainted by disagreements. Divers clearing a fisherman's nets found the submarine but while they negotiated over releasing the coordinates the remote sensing team independently located it.

The hull lies on the seabed and though damaged is intact. Since designation great effort has been put into ensuring effective management. There have been setbacks with reports of diver vandalism and damage from trawlers. Early searchers hoped to raise her but these ideas are now tempered by the experience with *Holland I*. However she is extremely vulnerable where she lies.

In 1997 a large collaborative project sought the information necessary for decision-making. The task was tackled by the Archaeological Diving Unit, a professional survey team and nearly one hundred volunteers coordinated by the Nautical Archaeology Society. They surveyed the structure of the hull and studied the colonising marine life. Remote sensing was used to search the area around the wreck for debris which could then be located, recorded and if necessary moved to safety.

Viewpoint: the wreck lies a considerable distance off Rhyl
Display: models and history: Merseyside Maritime Museum and the Royal Navy Submarine Museum
Further reading: Murphy, W. 1987. *The Life of Reverend George Garrett Pasha. Father of the Submarine* (historical)

144

Stern View

In 1965 the science writer Angela Croome summed up the opportunities and the dangers which confronted underwater archaeology:

> Only a ship assembles in such a small space so great an amount of evidence of the past; the trivial and the magnificent side by side in all the vividness of reality. The museums and archaeological institutes have been slow to grasp the prize being offered them. The laws governing larceny from the seabed leave many gaps open for the souvenir-hunter to wriggle through; also it is exceedingly difficult to put up fences on the bottom of the sea or to catch the culprit who has been poaching.

> The remarkable completeness of the picture that can be obtained if a wreck is systematically and scientifically explored is only now beginning to be appreciated. Whereas the science of land archaeology is over 100 years old, underwater archaeology is barely ten ... As underwater archaeology advances it will be possible to look further and further around the corner of history.

Chronological List of Historic Wrecks

Built	Ship		Lost	Ship
Before	-1100	Langdon Bay	-1100	Langdon Bay
Before	-1100	Moor Sand	-1100	Moor Sand
Before	1000	Erme Ingot	1000	Erme Ingot
	1060	Smalls	1060	Smalls
	1418	*Grace Dieu*	**1439**	*Grace Dieu*
	1500	Brighton Marina	1500	Gull Rock
	1500	Gull Rock	1500	Brighton Marina
	1509	*Mary Rose*	1520	Studland Bay
	1520	Studland Bay	**1527**	*St Anthony*
	1527	St Anthony	1530	Cattewater
	1530	Cattewater	1580	Dunwich Bank
	1540	Dunwich Bank	**1545**	*Mary Rose*
	1555	Bartholomew Ledge	1555	Bartholomew Ledge
	1567	Yarmouth Roads	1567	Yarmouth Roads
	1575	Pwll Fanog	1575	Pwll Fanog
	1580	Church Rocks	1580	Church Rocks
	1588	*Girona*	**1588**	*Girona*
	1603	Rill Cove	1603	Rill Cove
	1640	Salcombe Cannon	1640	Salcombe Cannon
	1640	Duart Point	**1653**	*Duart Point*
	1655	*Dartmouth*	**1664**	*Kennemerland*
	1660	*Mary*	**1675**	*Mary*
	1661	*Kennemerland*	**1684**	*Schiedam*
	1662	*Wrangels Palais*	**1687**	*Wrangels Palais*
	1678	*Stirling Castle*	**1689**	*Anne*
	1678	*Anne*	**1690**	*Coronation*
	1678	Tearing Ledge	**1690**	*Dartmouth*
	1678	*Restoration*	1700	Erme Estuary
	1679	*Northumberland*	1700	Rhinns of Islay
	1684	*Schiedam*	1702	Tal-y-Bont
	1685	*Coronation*	**1703**	*Stirling Castle*
	1694	Tearing Ledge	**1703**	*Restoration*
	1698	*Hazardous*	1707	Tearing Ledge
	1700	Erme Estuary	**1703**	*Northumberland*
	1700	Rhinns of Islay	**1706**	*Hazardous*
	1702	Tal-y-Bont		
	1709	*Royal Anne*	1721	*Royal Anne*
	1742	*Amsterdam*	**1743**	*Amsterdam*
	1744	*Invincible*	**1753**	*Assurance*
	1747	*Assurance*	**1758**	*Invincible*
	1763	*Hanover*	**1763**	*Hanover*
	1787	*Colossus*	1787	S. Edinb'gh Channel
	1787	S. Edinb'gh Channel	**1798**	*Colossus*
	1798	*Admiral Gardner*	1800	Seaton Carew
	1800	Seaton Carew	**1809**	*Admiral Gardner*
	1805	*Pomone*	**1811**	*Pomone*
	1863	*Iona II*	**1864**	*Iona II*
	1879	*Resurgam*	**1880**	*Resurgam*

In the lists above only the dates in bold type are certain, known from historical records. Chronological lists are unavoidably crude, based on current judgements of the available evidence. For unidentified sites, notional dates are deduced from the surviving remains. Few have sufficient structure for comparison with identified shipwrecks in other countries. Date-marked artefacts are helpful, such as naval equipment, coins, pewter and silverware. While the shipwreck must post-date these, they provide neither the year of build nor time of loss. The scope for error is apparent from the great age of some objects found on ships of known date. For many unidentified sites, dates can only be deduced by comparing recovered objects with established chronologies of similar artefacts.

The Danes led the way with legislation to protect their underwater sites. In the last three decades many countries in the northern and southern hemispheres have adopted blanket protection for shipwrecks over a certain age. Their national legislation safeguards the most international of heritage sites, ships of all countries. In the UK calls for protection of all wrecks more than 50 or 100 years old have been opposed by salvage and sport diving interests.

The Protection of Wrecks Act (1973) provided the mechanism to 'put up fences' around selected shipwrecks. In twenty-five years this has removed only forty-seven shipwreck sites from free public access. Very little of the UK seabed has been put out of bounds to divers, fishermen and other sea-users. The Historic Wreck exclusion zones range from 50 to 300m radius. The most common designation is a radius of 100m, roughly the size of a public monument such as the Tower of London. The total area of current exclusion zones is 830 acres (3.36km square), a little more than the overall area of Dover Harbour.

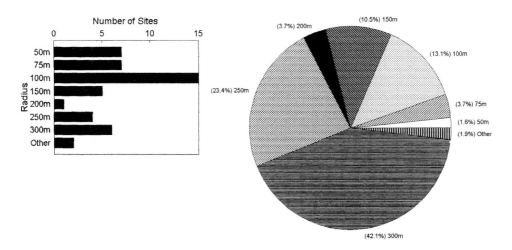

Forty-seven Historic Wrecks shown by size of exclusion zone.

Contribution of different size zones to the current overall protected area.

Predictions over the activities of poachers have proved all too true. It is not only treasure which attracts souvenir-hunters. In 1996 *Resurgam* was vandalised. 'Despite attempts to seal the conning tower ... in the week between the location of the vessel and the Designation Order being placed, portable items were taken off the submarine and the conning tower steering wheel was broken.' Many licencees are powerless against unauthorised divers and there is dismay that the Department for Culture Media and Sport have no active role in enforcing the exclusion zones which they impose. The three-year delay in designating the Salcombe Wreck shows that the rights of a salvor in possession are considered the more effective safeguard.

An inability to protect adequately the UK's Historic Wrecks fails the people of many countries who have a pride in their history. A ship can be built, owned and operated in different countries. In these three aspects documents show that the shipwrecks represent England, Scotland and Wales, America, Denmark, France, Italy, the Low Countries, Portugal, Spain and Sweden. Surviving cargo and the possessions of crew and passengers represent a far more numerous list of countries which stretch around the globe.

The forty-seven Historic Wrecks have led 'further and further around the corner of history'. The group spans an immense time period from the mid-twelfth century BC to AD 1880. The exceptional range of objects and information extracted from individual wrecks shows how much richer and more comprehensive an understanding of all periods could be gained if, survival and discovery permitting, Historic Wrecks could be protected for all periods. The current list is heavily biased to the late seventeenth/early eighteenth centuries.

Of the identified Historic Wrecks 44% were built in the seventeenth century with a further 32% and 12% in the eighteenth and nineteenth centuries. There are nine vessels, nearly one fifth of the total number of sites, which were certainly built between 1650 and 1700. Looking at both identified and unidentified Historic Wrecks, with only eight exceptions, they date between 1500 and 1800.

It is clear that the chronological distribution of the Historic Wrecks bears no relation to the number of ships built. The difficulty of locating early wrecks undoubtedly accounts for the few dating before 1500, but failure to designate explains the tailing off after 1750. It is from this date that the number of ships rapidly increased to carry the goods of industrialising Britain as she expanded and became the foremost shipping nation. Loss of these vessels is, however, reflected in the many shipwrecks located, but not protected, on the UK seabed.

Analysis of the National Inventory of Maritime Archaeology for England showed that, of the documented shipping casualties and known wrecks, over 90% were lost after 1750, with two-thirds of that number dating to after 1850. The chronological distribution of the Historic Wrecks is quite different, with only 28% lost after 1750. Until 1990 no steam vessels had been included and the latest date of build among Historic Wrecks was that of *Pomone*, 1805.

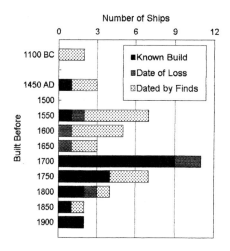

Identified Historic Wrecks by year of build.

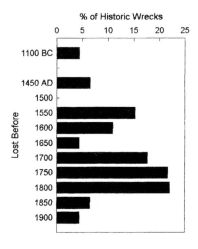

All Historic Wrecks (%) by year of loss.

The lack of chronological spead results in bias in the type of vessels which have been protected. There are only two wrecks from the era of steam, a submarine and a paddle-wheeled passenger steamer. Ship type can only be accurately assigned for well-documented shipwrecks. Nineteen vessels (twenty sites) were naval ships, designed for warfare or serving with naval forces, although their original function may have been different. There are three named East Indiamen. In addition to these armed ships, guns have been recovered from a further fifteen sites. Four sites comprise cargo which dates to the era before guns were invented.

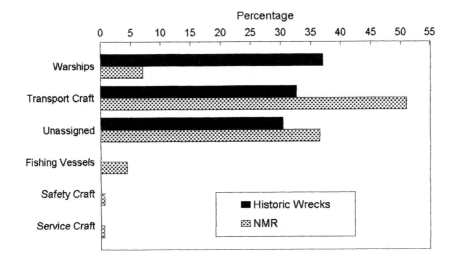

The National Inventory of Maritime Archaeology for England assigns a function to each shipwreck. This shows the numerical superiority of cargo and passenger ships providing 'transport'. This is not apparent when Historic Wrecks are similarly divided.

The Historic Wrecks give a good indication of where more shipwrecks can be found. Study has shown the range of preservation which can be expected from sites: in deep sand or mud such as *Amsterdam*, *Invincible*, *Mary Rose* and *Stirling Castle;* in shallow deposits such as *Dartmouth*, Studland Bay and Tal-y-Bont; or in rock gullies like *Colossus* and *Kennemerland*. Thirty-one Historic Wrecks are in the major shipping route, the English Channel, with clusters on well-known shipping hazards such as the Isles of Scilly, the Lizard and Goodwin Sands. The distribution of lighthouses is a good indicator of the existence of sea routes and such hazards. They often mark areas in which there have been many documented ship losses but which are entirely lacking in designations. A wider spread of Historic Wrecks could more evenly represent the incidence of ship loss, a facet of maritime history which, beyond its impact on individual human lives, was of considerable economic significance to the individuals and comunities which had committed their resources to building and lading the vessels.

The designation of Historic Wreck sites has been principally a reactive, *ad hoc* response to requests for the protection of individual vessels. The overall group does not represent

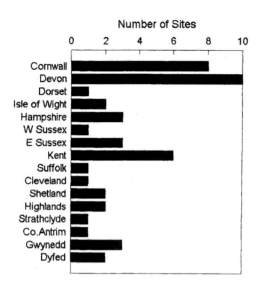

Number of Sites

Distribution of forty-seven Historic Wrecks by county.

the objective selection of either the most worthwhile or the most endangered of the many wrecks already located in UK waters. Analysis highlights the naivety of regarding the currently designated sites as an adequate sample of shipwrecks to represent the maritime past. From the outset administration of the 1973 Act was not accompanied by: resources to enforce protection; a management framework to ensure their investigation on a scientific basis; a commitment to automatic academic publication; and popular dissemination of the resulting information. A major shortcoming, despite the sympathetic and sensitive handling by the Receiver of Wreck, is the continuing legal requirement for artefacts to be dealt with like any other salvaged material.

How far the UK lags behind world opinion in the care of its Historic Wrecks has been highlighted by the *International Charter on the Protection and Management of the Underwater Cultural Heritage* ratified in 1996. It sets out as fundamental principles the importance of: preserving sites *in situ*; providing public access; and ensuring that investigation is based on research objectives, non-intrusive methods and full documentation. It denounces funding arrangements which require the sale of artefacts or their dispersal. It promotes interim reports on investigations and popular presentation in a range of media.

> 'Archaeology is a public activity: everybody is entitled to draw upon the
> past in informing their own lives, and every effort to curtail knowledge
> of the past is an infringemnt of personal autonomy.'

It is hoped that this book will show many people the richness of the UK's Historic Wrecks and that their voices will support future moves to improve the care and interpretation of shipwrecks for the benefit of all.

Through interpretation understanding, through understanding care. This wrecked notice, summer 1997, reflects the failure of successive government departments to promote the conservation of Historic Wrecks through interpretation for the whole community.

Glossary

Breech	rear portion of a gun where the charge was placed. Breech-loading guns had a separate chamber to hold the charge. Cattewater and Tal-Y Bont breech-loaders: Colour Plate 8; Tal-Y-Bont breech chamber p.123
Caulking	material forced between plank seams after assembly
Carvel	smooth outer planking without overlaps and fastened directly to frames
Clinker	overlapping outer planking, fastened plank-to-plank along their edges
Esmeril	small bronze breech-loading swivel gun with a bore of about 52mm (2in). *Girona* esmeril: Colour Plate 5a
Frame	transverse assembly of several pieces of timber to strengthen the hull
Garboard strake	the line of planks adjacent to the keel
Keelson	beam lying along the centre of the vessel to provide longitudinal strength, usually fitted over the frames and a seating for one or more masts. *Cattewater* keelson: p. 43
Lateen	a narrow triangular sail set on a very long yard
Minion	bronze 4-pounder gun firing shot with a diameter of about 3in (76mm). Church Rocks minion: Colour Plate 8
Nocturnal	instrument first described in 1581 for measuring the time of night by means of the stars.
Rib	one-piece transverse strengthening member fitted inside the planking of a vessel
Rove	small plate or ring on which the point of a nail is deformed to create a rivet
Saker	bronze 5-pounder gun firing shot with a diameter of about 3.5in (89mm). Dunwich Bank saker: Colour Plate 9
Transom	stern terminating in transverse planking
Treenail	round wooden fastening in a pre-drilled hole. The end is sometimes split and a small wedge inserted to ensure a tight fit

Further Introductory Reading

Most readable introduction to key underwater discoveries, their investigation and place in history:
Throckmorton, P. (ed.) 1987. *History from the Sea. Shipwrecks and Archaeology*. Mitchell Beazley

A classic explanation of the construction of traditional craft and how they are built to suit the sea conditions in different areas of Britain:
McKee, E. 1998. *Working Boats of Britain. Their Shape and Purpose*. Conway Maritime Press.

Wooden ship construction explained with delightful pencil illustrations by a traditional boatbuilder in:
Frost, T. 1987. *From Tree to Sea. Building A Wooden Steam Drifter*. Terence Dalton.

Further Reading for Reference

The only published account of the annual working of the Protection of Wrecks Act is:
Advisory Committee on Historic Wreck Sites. 1997. *Annual Report 1996*. (Available from the Department for Culture, Media and Sport).

The standards expected of underwater archaeology across the world are set out in:
International Council on Monuments and Sites. *International Charter on the Protection and Management of Underwater Cultural Heritage*. (Available from ICOMOS UK, 10 Barley Mow Passage, London, W4 4PH).

Catalogue of known shipwrecks round Great Britain, of which three volumes have been published to date, covering the coast from North Devon anticlockwise to Northumberland:
Larn, R. & B. 1995 - . *Shipwreck Index of the British Isles*. Lloyds Register of Shipping.

Well-illustrated information on underwater archaeology world-wide:
Delgado, P. (ed.) 1997. *British Museum Encyclopaedia of Underwater and Maritime Archaeology*. British Museum Press.

The most up-to-date list of published information:
Illsley, J. 1996. *An Indexed Bibliography of Underwater Archaeology and Related Topics*. Anthony Nelson.

Papers on the contribution of shipwrecks to knowledge of the past:
Redknap, M.(ed.) 1997. *Artefacts from Wrecks. Dated Assemblages from the Late Middle Ages to the Industrial Revolution*. Oxbow Monograph 38.

A handbook on the basics of underwater archaeology:
Dean, M. *et al.* 1992. *Archaeology Underwater. The NAS Guide to Principles and Practice*. Nautical Archaeology Society and Archetype Publications.

Addresses

British Museum, Great Russell Street, London, WC1B 3DG

Chatham Historic Dockyard, Chatham, ME4 4TE

Dover Museum, Market Square, Dover, CT16 1PB

Great Britain, Great Western Dock, Gas ferry Road, Bristol, BS1 6TY

Islay Museum Trust, c/o Islay Life, Port Charlotte, Islay, Scotland

McClean Museum & Art Gallery, Central Library, Clyde Square, Greenock, PA15 1NA

Mary Rose Museum, HM Naval Base, Portsmouth, PO1 3LX

Merseyside Maritime Museum, Albert Dock, Liverpool, L3 4AQ

National Maritime Museum, Greenwich. London. SE10 9NF

National Museums of Scotland, Chambers Street, Edinburgh, EH1 1JF.

National Museum of Wales, Cathays Park, Cardiff, CF1 3NP.

Paddle Steamer Preservation Society, PO Box 385, Hazlemere, High Wycombe, HP11 1AG

Penzance Maritime Museum, 19 Chapel Street, Penzance, TR18 4AF

Poole Maritime Museum, The Quay, Poole, Dorset

Plymouth City Museum, Drake's Circus, Plymouth, PL4 8AJ

Porthleven Wreck & Rescue, The Quay, Porthleven, Helston, Cornwall

Ramsgate Maritime Museum, Clock House, Pier Yard, Royal Harbour, Ramsgate, CT11 8LS

Royal Albert Memorial Museum, Queen Street, Exeter. EX4 3RX

Royal Armouries, Armouries Drive, Leeds, LS10 1LT

Royal Naval Museum, HM Naval Base, Portsmouth, PO1 3LX

Royal Navy Submarine Museum, Haslar Jetty, Gosport, PO12 2AS

St Mary's Museum, Church Street, St Mary's, Isles of Scilly, TR21 0JT

Shetland Museum, Lower Hilhead, Lerwick, Shetland, ZE10 0EL

Shipwreck & Heritage Centre, Charlestown, St Austell, PL25 3NN

Shipwreck Heritage Centre, Rock-a-Nore Road, Hastings, TN4 3DW

Southampton Maritime Museum, Wool House, Bugle Street, Southampton

Suffolk Underwater Studies, Front Street, Orford, IP12 2LN

Teignmouth Museum, 29 French Street, Teignmouth, TQ14 8ST

Trincomalee, Hartlepool Historic Quay, Maritime Avenue, Hartlepool

Unicorn, Victoria Dock, Dundee, DD1 3JA

The Ulster Museum, Botanic Gardens, Belfast, BT9 5AB

Victory, HM Naval Base, Portsmouth, PO1 3LX.

VOC-Schip Amsterdam, Postbus 18257, 1001 ZD, Amsterdam.

Advisory Committee on Historic Wreck Sites, 3rd Floor, Department for Culture Media & Sport, 2-4 Cockspur Street, London, SW1Y 5DH.

Cadw: Welsh Historic Monuments, Crown Building, Cathays Park, Cardiff, CF1 3NQ.

Historic Scotland, Longmore House, Salisbury Place, Edinburgh, EH9 1SH.

Environment and Heritage Service, 5-33 Hill Street, Belfast, BT1 2LA.

Royal Commission on the Historic Monuments of England, Public Services, National Monuments Record Centre, Kemble Drive, Swindon, SN2 2GZ.

Royal Commission for the Ancient & Historic Monuments of Scotland, John Sinclair House, 16 Bernard Terrace, Edinburgh, EH8 9NX.

Royal Commission for the Ancient & Historic Monuments of Wales, National Monuments Record, Crown Building, Plas Crug, Aberystwyth, Ceredigion, SY23 1NJ.

Receiver of Wreck, The Coastguard Agency, Spring Place, 105 Commercial Road, Southampton, SO15 1EG.

Nautical Archaeology Society, c/o Fort Cumberland, Fort Cumberland Rd, Eastney, Portsmouth, PO4 9LD.

Index

Within this general index there are the following headings: artefacts; cargoes & ballast; Historic Wrecks; museums; organisations; places; ship/wreck names; ships structure; and ship types.